To Bob Brown

Merry Christmas 2000

Chuck Cuch

A Democrat Looks at His Party

DEAN ACHESON

A DEMOCRAT LOOKS AT HIS PARTY

GREENWOOD PRESS, PUBLISHERS
WESTPORT, CONNECTICUT

Library of Congress Cataloging in Publication Data

Acheson, Dean Gooderham, 1893-1971.
A Democrat looks at his party.

Reprint of the 1st ed. published by Harper, New
York.
1. Democratic Party. 2. United States--Poli-
tics and government--20th century. I. Title.
JK2316.A25 1976   329.3'009'045   76-48254
ISBN 0-8371-9332-X

Originally published in 1955 by Harper & Brothers, New York

Reprinted with the permission of Harper & Row, Publishers, Inc.

Reprinted in 1976 by Greenwood Press, Inc.

Library of Congress Catalog Card Number   76-48254

ISBN 0-8371-9332-X

Printed in the United States of America

*And it seems to me that at this time
we need education in the obvious
more than investigation of the obscure.*
OLIVER WENDELL HOLMES, JR.

Contents

A Democrat Looks at His Party

1

Personal Prologue

SOME years ago I spent a week or more in a distant
city on a law case. My client and I—he would have
been described by our weekly press as a tycoon, and a
tycoon of the blood royal—shared a hotel suite. In addition to his lofty business status, this man was charming,
firm in his views, but with deep curiosity and a bent for
speculative inquiry. We spent many evenings together,
and as he sank more deeply into his chair, sucked at his
pipe, and sparingly quenched his thirst, the talk rambled
where it would.

One evening, after a pause in which he seemed weighing a decision, he said, "May I ask you a rather blunt
question?" I told him to fire when he was ready. He
went on:

"You are counsel for my company. Let us say, to minimize the personal side, that this means you are intelligent and experienced. And yet you are a Democrat. How can this be?" It was quite clear that this was not an invitation to an argument, but to explore together what was to him a puzzling problem of human behavior.

For some evenings we explored it, not sticking on points on which after examination our views remained divergent, but noting them and pushing on further into the heart of the matter. No soul was saved, or sought to be saved, from the burning, but both of us were enlightened. Certainly I was, as any man must be by an examination of his premises and prejudices—those prejudgments which all of us must make on matters where our knowledge always remains imperfect and incomplete. Years full of "the sundry and manifold changes of the world," as the Collect puts it, have passed since I shared this experience with my client. Yet the current of thought begun with him has gone on. It now finds an outlet in this writing, which is not an apologia, nor a party pamphlet, nor a history. Rather it draws from personal and public experience, remote and current, some general ideas which might explain why a man gave, and continues to give, his loyalty to the Democratic party, which might explain something of the nature of the party itself, of what it has achieved in the course of its long history, and of what it must still achieve if, in our political folklore, it is to continue to be called, "Old Indestructible."

Each of us reaches his political affiliation or faith, if one prefers a word more weighted with imponderables, by diverse routes: some by birth and inescapable circumstance; some by more direct revelation of interest, material or otherwise; others through intellectual appraisal of the public good and of the merits of the competitors who claim the opportunity to serve it. But still others, whether they are many or few I do not know, have by some accident of time, chance, or receptiveness been tuned to respond to a note of leadership as clear, at least so it seemed at the time, as Roland's horn at Roncesvalles.

At any rate, at the beginning of the second decade of this century, when the world seemed young and I certainly was, I thrilled to every bugle call to action blown by the "Young Turks," the "Progressives," and most of all by "T.R.," the most ebullient of them all, in the revolt against the "Old Guard," the "malefactors of great wealth," against "reaction" in the person of Uncle Joe Cannon and inaction in the benign and ineffective figure of President William Howard Taft. It was springtime and "T.R." rode again. I for certain would not be one of those who—

now abed
Shall think themselves accurs'd they were not here,
And hold their manhoods cheap whiles any speaks
That fought with us upon Saint Crispin's day.

Political parties mattered little. The fight and the leaders mattered much. At least so it all seemed to one youth a long time ago. Perhaps there was a good deal of what would later be called Hollywood about it all. Perhaps those glittering leaders were engaged in a shrewder play for party control than the followers and water boys understood. Undoubtedly, deeper still, all the actors were profoundly ignorant of the realities of the world in which they lived—a world rushing with fearful speed to 1914 and forty years of intermittent war, of revolution and realignment. At all events in almost a moment the glamorous cavalcade had vanished. In one way nothing of it remained; in another, nothing would ever again be quite the same, as in a forest after a hurricane all the trees lean the same way.

But for one who remained the political landscape was not empty. A new figure had emerged, leading a solid and rejuvenated party—and rejuvenated in no small way by an infusion of Bull Moose blood. For it is good Jeffersonian doctrine that "a little rebellion now and then is a good thing."[1] As the decade went on and I passed, in Duff-Cooper's classification of the ages of man, from boyhood to youth, the quality and power of Mr. Wilson's leadership and the significance of the party he led became clearer and more compelling. Few of the doc-

---

[1] Letter to James Madison, 1787, *The Writings of Thomas Jefferson* (G. P. Putnam's Sons, New York, Ford Ed., 1892-99), Vol. IV, p. 362.

trines of the New Freedom were new, and none were glamorous. But, if the key was lower, the composition was more solid. If the President was austere, there also played around him the lightning flashes of insight and inspiration. As the shocks and problems of the war came and gave way to the even greater problems of the peace, he became a towering figure. If his mistakes were great and tragic, as Maynard Keynes pointed out, great also was his understanding of the new role which his country must play in the realignment of power which the crumbling of empires and emergence of new forces necessitated.

In 1920 it all ended in the collapse and twilight and darkness of a Götterdämmerung. Warren Harding was "restored" by the Senate allies like a Louis XVIII, except that, unlike the Bourbons, the Old Guard had learned nothing and forgotten everything. For one man, as for many, loyalties and beliefs were tempered and hardened by a decade of political eclipse. I had become a Democrat.

T.R.'s call to arms had started me on a long journey. Along the way there was no blinding light or voice speaking such as Saul experienced on the road to Damascus. But rather the growth of an awareness of belonging, as one on emerging from childhood becomes aware of belonging in one's family, or as one becomes aware of being an American. But these similes are in one respect misleading and defective. They leave out the element of choice. It was not a choice made dramatically and at one time. The choice developed like the awareness which I have mentioned. And, as in these fellowships of family and country, all was not rosy. There was little cause for pride in the Democratic convention of 1924 and the infection of Know Nothingism and Ku Klux Klanism of which it was a symptom, an infection which, like the hookworm, the party seemed to have picked up through the feet and not through the head or heart. But the party's troubles were not a cause, so it seemed to me, for turning from it. They were one's own troubles to be lived through and cured.

But those parched and weary years were not without a source of refreshment and inspiration. Al Smith in New York, the Happy Warrior in the brown derby, brought humanity to administration and common sense and the facts to political debate, as he would say, "Well, let's look at the record." His campaign song, "The Sidewalks of New York," still moves me as "Dixie" moves a Southerner, and no Highlander welcomed the return of Bonnie Prince Charlie more enthusiastically than I welcomed Al Smith's nomination for the Presidency in 1928. And with about the same results.

2

The Oldest Party

Is the Youngest Party

IT IS ONE thing, however, to explain one's entrance
into a fellowship. It is another to expound the reasons
for remaining in it throughout the years. How is it that
so vast a number of us have done this and still do it?
However we become Democrats, why do we remain
Democrats?

When a Democrat looks into his party, he learns, to
start with, that he belongs to the oldest political party
in the world. This comes as something of a shock. For
the party around him has all the attributes of youth and
vitality. But none the less, it is the oldest in the world.
True, the Conservative party in England can put in a
claim, but the weight of the evidence is against it.

The birthday of the Democratic party is usually given

as May 23, 1792, the date of a letter from Mr. Jefferson to General Washington[1] giving the name to the party which the former then led. The date is fairly supportable, though it may be criticized as pushing things a bit. But certainly by the election of 1794 the party was firmly established and in the field. Its formal and full name in the early days was the Democratic-Republican party. But the noxious suffix was dropped in 1828—though here and there one finds a Democrat who does not seem to have heard of the improvement and gets confused.

In England the Conservative party adopted its name in 1835, but fairness demands the admission that the party is older than the name. Lord Hugh Cecil says that "It is picturesque and not untrue to fix a particular day as the birthday of Conservatism."[2] The day chosen is May 6, 1790. On that day Burke rose in the House of Commons, then discussing the Quebec bill, to make a speech on the French Revolution. Fox raised a point of order which was sustained. During the debate a bitter quarrel regarding the Revolution took place between these intimate personal and political friends which ended their friendship and forecast a new division in British politics.

[1] Letter to George Washington, May 23, 1792, *The Writings of Thomas Jefferson* (The Thomas Jefferson Memorial Association, Washington, D.C., 1903), Vol. VIII, pp. 341, 344-345.

[2] Lord Hugh Cecil, *Conservatism* (Henry Holt and Company, Home University Library, New York, 1919), p. 42.

On this foundation Lord Hugh rests the observation "Conservatism may be said to have been born"[3] in 1790. In doing so, I think he "stands upon a ledge too narrow for safety." If he had said "conceived," yes; but "born," no. For Burke's *Reflections on the French Revolution,* which established the intellectual foundations of British Conservatism, was not to have its full effect for some years yet. And one would be hard pressed to find, before Pitt's second ministry and the resumption of the war with Napoleon in 1804, the confluence of the principal streams which joined to make Conservatism—the Tory tradition of support of King and Church, the imperialism of Chatham, and the fear of the French Revolution.

However this may be, enough has been said to show that the Democratic claim is the stronger one but that our British friends are most ancient and honorable contenders.

While one takes pride, one does not linger over this ancient lineage. For one is again struck by the paradox that the oldest party has at the same time all the marks of youth. How has it lasted so long and remained so young? For youthful it surely is. It is turbulent. It is disorderly. It is adventurous, imaginative, more governed by hopes than fears. And it has another special characteristic of youth. It responds to leadership of strong and vibrant personalities, who so often have come to the fore

[3] *Ibid.,* p. 44.

through its own virile processes. These leaders have re-shaped and redirected the party to meet the emerging problems of each new era. The history of the party is in large part the history of them—of Jefferson, Jackson, Wilson, Franklin Roosevelt, and, unless we are too close, and I am too warped by affection for judgment, Harry S. Truman. Each of these has left his special imprint on the party, its traditions, and its policies.

Although each imprint is special, each has used the precedents of the past in meeting the needs of the present and so given continuity to the search for progress in order, for liberty in tradition, for a sense of life in form, as the great judge-developers have given to the common law. Indeed, the history of the party is the history of America's unwritten constitution, of the powers of the federal government, of the nature and authority of the Presidential office and its relation to the legislative and judicial powers. However separated or close in time, these great of the party appear to us side by side. For each, supported by those who had gone before, so managed what was novel to the moment that the effect of the innovation, however great, appeared to be and often was the flowering of what another had planted.

If, in contrast, one turns to the great of the Republican party, one sees how strangely they have left no mark on party policy. There was the glorious moment of Abraham Lincoln, and the lesser, but still major, moment of Theodore Roosevelt. But what each ventured to do shared a common end. Almost before Lincoln was cold in his grave, his unhappy successor—and Lincoln's policies with him—were overwhelmed by the bitter hatred of the Radical Republicans for both. So, too, was Theodore Roosevelt and his "Square Deal" treated by the Republicans of a later day, as if regicide was the first duty of the faithful. Even now, with reference to Lincoln's policies—though not to Theodore Roosevelt's whose mere name suggests a wild man in Republican mythology—one can see more than a passing resemblance between Republican outlook and that attributed by fable to the people of Siena. In the time of the Renaissance—so the fable goes—they had hired a captain to wage war on a neighboring town, and after his victory, the Sienese met to consider how they could best reward a man who had served them well in a foreign contest, but was now favorably placed to conquer his original employers. No plan joining prudence to gratitude seemed quite satisfactory until it was proposed that the captain should be killed and then worshiped as Siena's patron saint. The suggestion was carried by acclamation, and no time was lost in putting it into effect.

The disconnection between the great figures of the Republican party and the body of the party itself is such a recurrent phenomenon as to suggest permanent underlying causes. One of them, at least, is the chronic inclination of the party to divorce power from responsibility, and set each on an independent career of its own. In the name of checking the danger of "executive aggrandizements," the party historically would subordinate the Executive to the Congress, and the national voice to a babel of local voices. It would have a Legislature with great powers and few responsibilities, and an Executive with few powers and great responsibilities. Such an arrangement is not without its allure within the political, military, economic, and social community, for it permits the Legislature to grant subsidies, emoluments, immunities, and privileges, while the real authors of the mischief are lost in the crowd. The people are baffled to know on whom to fix the blame, though their injuries are plain enough.

In Republican ranks there is a recurrent inclination to view government itself as being but an administrative process, like good bookkeeping. Thus the sum of the Republican political consciousness, in the second Hoover Commission, for instance, often comes to be limited to the prospect of "getting one hundred cents on every dollar that is spent." So far as it goes, this aim is worthy enough. But that government is also a process by which great social projects—each a manifestation of the age-old questions of human happiness and political justice—are brought forth for discussion, if noticed at all, is excoriated as in the report on development of power resources. There is here no sense of adventure, of the drama or the gaiety of the democratic march; no sense of generation and regeneration, looking beyond that which is to that which shall be. A politics from which all this is lacking can raise great relics. It cannot very well raise a race of men wherein fathers feel they have done well if their sons do better.

But to return to the Democratic party, one asks again, where do its enduring qualities come from? At what fountain of youth does this lusty old party drink? We are told that at sixty every man is responsible for his face. Some, we might add, could be convicted at an earlier age. So, I think, a political party's mode of life determines its state of health and the state of its constitution.

From the very beginning the Democratic party has been broadly based. If we can think freshly through a tired word, it has been the party of the many. These were the urban worker; the backwoods merchant and banker; the small farmer, whether he was a cotton, tobacco, or grain grower; the large landholders of the South, who saw themselves being milked by the commercial and financial magnates gathered under Hamilton's banner; the newly arrived immigrants—then chiefly Scotch-Irish—who were peopling the western wilderness, and who saw in Jefferson's party, the party of the underdog. (These Scotch-Irish, incidentally, men of "long-limbs, long knives, long guns and long memories," were called "foreign savages" and "liars" by the Federalists. And it was to curb the accretions of strength they gave the Jeffersonian cause, as they took possession of the wilderness, that the Alien part of the Alien and Sedition Laws was explicitly framed later on.) Besides this human composition, from the very outset, the Jeffersonians represented an interregional alliance, with one anchor in Virginia, another in New York, and still another in western Pennsylvania. In the course of arbitrating their natural differences, localisms were changed into a national party outlook.

The party's earliest efforts were to bring the many into control of government through the extension of the franchise and through frequent elections in state and nation to make the voter, thus multiplied, sovereign. This is what the word democracy meant from its Greek roots— the people's rule—until Communist dialectic sought to turn it into its opposite. Now this somewhat hackneyed observation is not meant to conclude the discussion by surrounding the party with a moral and emotional halo. Many people are not necessarily more right, or wiser, or more devoted to the public good than a few people. But, in considering the attributes of a political association formed and conducted to gain control of and to carry on government, the many have an important and most relevant characteristic. They have many interests, many points of view, many purposes to accomplish, and a party which represents them will have their many interests, many points of view, and many purposes also. It is this multiplicity of interests which, I submit, is the principal clue in understanding the vitality and endurance of the Democratic party.

This becomes clearer when we consider that the Democratic party has survived two opponents and now faces a third, all of which have represented not many interests but pretty much a single dominating interest. The base of all three opponents has been the interest of the economically powerful, of those who manage affairs, of those who own property in its most important manifestation from time to time. I say, "in its most important manifestation," because property covers everything from one's shoes to the blue-chip stocks on the Exchange, and in the hierarchy of property the primacy has shifted three times in the long history of the Democratic party and its three opponents. The dichotomy has not been between a party of property and a party of proletarians, sans-culottes, or descamisados. It has been between a party which centers on the interests deriving from property in its most important form and a party of many interests, including property interests.

For instance, until the end of the eighteenth century, the dominant form of property was land. General Washington was a rich man and he was rich in land. Land was what the powerful sought for and acquired. By the first quarter of the next century the primacy had pretty well shifted to trading ventures and promotion—trading in goods, trading in land, and trading in shares, shares in land companies, bridge companies, banks, and so on. John Jacob Astor was a trader, and when he invested in land, it was in urban real estate. Manufacturing there was. But the "manufacturing interest" of which Hamilton spoke was not the same in form, grandeur, and power as that which was to come.

A new leader in the world of property emerged in the latter part of the nineteenth century and has since come to full flower. This is industry, production on a grand and massive scale with its attendant services of merchandising, finance, law, and advertising. It is all summed up in the word business and the dukes and princes of business are the leaders of big business.

The economic base and the principal interest of the Republican party is business. I hasten to add that I do not make this statement on my own authority. Mr. Gordon Harrison in his book, *Road to the Right,* subtitled "The Tradition and Hope of American Conservatism,"[4] asserts confidently and proudly (p. 310):

But the [Republican] party does stand for something—by and large for the dominant interests of the business community and for the business point of view. For better or worse American conservatism must build on its business base, and the root problem is not what the Republicans stand for

[4] William Morrow and Co., New York, 1954.

but what business stands for, not where the party may wish to go but where business politically is going.

Indeed, the present Administration describes itself as a business administration—in the words of Secretary of the Interior McKay, "an Administration representing business and industry."[5]

This business base of the Republican party is stressed not in any spirit of criticism. The importance of business is an outstanding fact of American life. Its achievements have been phenomenal. It is altogether appropriate that one of the major parties should represent its interests and points of view. It is stressed because here lies the significant difference between the parties, the single-interest party against the many-interest party, rather than in a supposed division by attitudes of mind, a conservative approach against a liberal approach. Some people are naturally more apprehensive of the unknown and untried than others. And, by the same token, some are more willing to experiment, more empirical, less bound by tradition and accepted notions than their fellows. But, by and large, the nature of one's interests is more likely to induce these bents of mind than the bents of mind to develop one's interests.

Carrying this difference between the parties further,

[5] Secretary Douglas McKay, before the Annual Meeting of the U.S. Chamber of Commerce, Washington, April 29, 1953, as reported in the Los Angeles *Times*, April 30, 1953, AP dispatch.

it has a bearing on preparation for the peculiar tasks of government—the art of government, despite the political scientists. For a business administration is more than apt, it is almost certain, to recruit its personnel from the ranks of business. As Mr. W. Randolph Burgess, at that time Deputy to the Secretary of the Treasury, formerly of the National City Bank, is reported to have said: ". . . our kind of people are now in power."[6] Business is different from government. The late Senator Taft understood this very well. "I'm not at all sure that all these businessmen are going to work out," he observed. "I don't know of any reason why success in business should mean success in public service."[7] One saw this during the last war when, despite the invaluable services rendered by many businessmen in tasks requiring business and technical knowledge, they so often floundered in positions of administrative responsibility in a political environment.

Public life, as Senator Taft was aware, is a new and untried medium for the businessman. He may do well but previous business success gives no assurance of it. The rules and customs he mastered in his private enterprise are virtually useless to him.[8] He is not free to buy

[6] Under Secretary of the Treasury W. Randolph Burgess, "Today's Monetary Policy," lecture delivered at Graduate School of Banking, Rutgers University, New Brunswick, N.J., June 12, 1953.

[7] Richard H. Rovere, "What Course for the Powerful Mr. Taft?" New York Times Magazine, March 22, 1953, pp. 9, 34.

[8] The summary statement about the nature of the businessman in government is drawn from Sidney Hyman's book, The American President (Harper & Brothers, New York, 1954), pp. 211-212.

and sell, to hire and fire. What he does is delineated by
Congress, ruled by the courts, guided and directed by the
President in the light of political exigencies. He is thrown
in with a group of men who, for the most part, are
strangers to him. He can hire a few people and dismiss a
few others. But he can neither engage nor "lay off" the
many thousands in a department or agency. They are
there by the permission of the Congress, under the sanction of the party patronage systems, and under the protection of the Civil Service Commission. Nor does the businessman in government deal, as formerly, in measurable
impersonal things. He deals in human beings, in their constantly changing values and aspirations, registered, in the
end, not by a profit-and-loss sheet expressed in dollars
and cents. They are registered in terms of victory or defeat, expressed in votes. He has no profit index to judge
his competence. Whether he is competent or incom-
petent, he can be repudiated in the first case and extolled
in the second, depending on the tone of political forces
in collision. He can draw flawless blueprints of how
things should be done. He has none of the coercive in-
struments he formerly used to make plans work in his
business. To survive in government, the businessman has
to be gifted in the art of political combination based on
consent; and a money-making art is no apprenticeship
for this larger challenge.

On the other hand, the processes of a party of many
interests are the very processes of government itself, and

experience in the management of such a party is apprenticeship in the art of government, the regulation and harmonization of various interests. Madison pointed out the nature of the task in the tenth number of *The Federalist:*

Those who hold and those who are without property have ever formed distinct interests in society. Those who are creditors, and those who are debtors, fall under a like discrimination. A landed interest, a manufacturing interest, a mercantile interest, a moneyed interest, with many lesser interests, grow up of necessity in civilized nations, and divide them into different classes, actuated by different sentiments and views. The regulation of these various and interfering interests forms the principal task of modern legislation, and involves the spirit of party and faction in the necessary and ordinary operations of the government.[9]

Policies and programs within the party must be developed in which no single interest is permitted to dominate the others. Labor, organized and unorganized, skilled and unskilled; white-collar workers, farmers, professional people; persons dependent on savings or pensions; intellectuals; people in search of housing or some minimum medical care; as well as businessmen—all these crisscrossing groups have interests and points of view which insistently demand attention and which in themselves

[9] James Madison, *The Federalist*, No. X (M. Walter Dunne, New York, 1901), Vol. I, pp. 62, 64-65.

form a rudimentary system of checks and balances. This becomes all the more so when we recall that the many-interest party covers all geographical areas of the country, while the other, for historical reasons, does not.

Here again the party is performing the function of restraint and compromise in the unwritten constitution. Calhoun described the need and the method, writing to support a quite different thesis but in words that contain wisdom and warning.

... there are [he said], two different modes in which the sense of the community may be taken: one, simply by the right of suffrage, unaided; the other, by the right through a proper organism. Each collects the sense of the majority. But one regards numbers only, and considers the whole community as a unit, having but one common interest throughout; and collects the sense of the greater number of the whole, as that of the community. The other, on the contrary, regards interests as well as numbers;—considering the community as made up of different and conflicting interests, as far as the action of the government is concerned; and takes the sense of each, through its majority or appropriate organ, and the united sense of all, as the sense of the entire community. The former of these I shall call the numerical, or absolute majority; and the latter, the concurrent, or constitutional majority.

... as there can be no constitution without the negative power, and no negative power without the concurrent majority—it follows, necessarily, that where the numerical majority has the sole control of the government, there can be no constitution; as constitution implies limitation or restriction,—and, of course, is inconsistent with the idea of sole or exclusive power. And hence, the numerical, unmixed with the concurrent majority, necessarily forms, in all cases, absolute government.[10]

If all of the interests which are comprised in the Democratic party were fragmented into separate parties and spent their impact directly on the legislative body, the result might well be either the irresolution and narrowness of electoral will which frustrates the accomplishment of national purposes in France, or the submersion of these many interests by a dominant one. This latter is, perhaps, what the Russians think they see when they refer to "the ruling circles in the United States." But the Democratic party performs through its own processes a preliminary accommodation and regulation of various and different interests before the legislative process begins, or as part of it, and by this develops policies and programs national in their scope and base.

There is another highly relevant characteristic of this diverse association covering so many different areas, interests, types of supporters, and points of view. A personality which can gain acceptance of his leadership in

[10] "A Disquisition on Government," *The Works of John C. Calhoun* (A. S. Johnston, Columbia, S.C., 1851), Vol. I, pp. 28, 36.

this party is apt to be a strong one, one calculated to win national acceptance and one equipped to exercise national leadership. Now, I know that there is eminent authority for the view that our political party system operates to present nonentities to the voters as Presidential candidates, men who by virtue of being such have given offense to none of the important and disparate groups which make up our electorate. De Tocqueville thought this—though why he should have in 1832 puzzles me. An instance of the delightful irony of history occurs in the words with which Woodrow Wilson agreed with him in 1885.

... so, when the presidential candidate came to be chosen, it was recognized as imperatively necessary that he should have as short a political record as possible, and that he should wear a clean and irreproachable insignificance. . . . A decisive career which gives a man a well-understood place in public estimation constitutes a positive disability for the presidency; because candidacy must precede election, and the shoals of candidacy can be passed only by a light boat which carries little freight and can be turned readily about to suit the intricacies of the passage.[11]

How much truth there is in this view we all know. So far as the Whig and Republican parties are concerned, it seems to have been vitiated only by inadvertence—

[11] Woodrow Wilson, *Congressional Government* (Houghton Mifflin Company, Boston, 1885), pp. 42-43.

through sheer error of judgment in appraising Lincoln, and by Czolgosz's bullet in the case of Theodore Roosevelt. Among the many-interest groups of the Democratic party when it is out of power there is no dominating management. It is much more open for the emergence of a strong personality and much more likely to respond to one, even when, as with William Jennings Bryan, it is led in enthusiasm to futility. Surely it has had its Alton B. Parker, but there is far less likelihood of the "selection" of a leader to provide a respectable front for the exercise of power by others, a William McKinley, a Warren Harding, or a Calvin Coolidge.

Perhaps it is for these reasons—the broad base of acceptability and confidence, the strong imaginative and often empirical qualities of its leaders, the definite conservative influence of many of its adherents—and not by chance that the Democratic party has piloted the country through periods of turmoil which have presented grave dangers in a wider area. It was the party of Jefferson and his successors which absorbed the shocks of the French Revolution and the Napoleonic Wars. The party of Jackson met those of the Industrial Revolution and the troubles which led in Europe to the revolutions of 1848. And the party of Franklin Roosevelt led the country, with its institutions unimpaired, through the great depression exacerbated by the dangers which the Russian Revolution and the growth of totalitarianism represented.

Its broad base and acceptability brought confidence to the many that their interests were appreciated. Its empiricism gave freedom to employ heterodox methods if they seemed to be useful. Its conservatism never let the experimentation get out of hand. When the ship righted after these hurricanes, all the ship's company were present and in good shape.

But, one may say, what about the years leading up to the Civil War? What sort of leadership was furnished by the Democratic party in the 1840's and 1850's? The point is well taken and should lead to modesty in the assertion of partisan claims. The kindest that can be said is that the leadership was mediocre—all leadership, Democratic and Whig; that of the great figures on the Hill, Webster, Calhoun, Clay; and of the lesser figures in the White House, the Whigs, Tyler and Fillmore, and the Democrats, Polk, Pierce, with all his gifts and charm, and the ineffective and distraught Buchanan.

Perhaps the conflicts developed by the passions and wills of the millions who were occupying and developing this continent were beyond the power of politicians and statesmen to channel into peaceful accommodation and eventual resolution. The drive to the Pacific Coast was both absorbing of interest and energy and opened a host of issues about the society which should exist in the new territory. The tariff issue threatened the cotton economy of the South, faced with exhausted land and an increasing demand for cotton for Eli Whitney's cotton gins. The financial chaos following the end of the Second Bank of the United States added to the bitterness and complexity of the sectional differences. And over all hung the ominous shift of power foreshadowed by the great growth of population and industry in the North.

All of these conflicts contributed to, and more and more found their expression in, the issue of slavery. And here one is torn between two lines of thought. On the one hand the problems were enormously complicated and difficult. Apart from the problem of slavery, they aroused the deepest passions of acquisitiveness and the possession of power. As the years went on, these passions mounted, under the lash of the slavery agitation, to fanaticism. Were they not beyond the capacity and understanding of the political managers? Is it reasonable to expect more of this period than what the Beards have called "The politics of the economic drift"?

But then one asks, was it beyond the capacity of political management at some time in these critical years to separate out the issue of slavery and to deal with it without war? Eminent Southerners from Jefferson to Tyler had looked forward to the elimination of slavery by gradual and orderly processes. Time, as well as economic and moral pressures, was on that side. In both North and South the narrow issue was developed and forced by small minorities. By the time of the Civil War the enrollment of slaveholders, large and small, in the South was 350,000—an important minority politically and socially, but not representative of the basic interests of the majority in the South. And in the North the Abolitionists were an even smaller minority—again dedicated and able, but not representative. Each carried on the most intense propaganda and even intimidation. But was the "irrepressible conflict" really irrepressible? Was there not a time when a political solution was possible between 1832, when Andrew Jackson dealt with nullification, and 1852, when Franklin Pierce carried every state but four on a pro-slavery platform? Perhaps not, but one fights against the conclusion. At least we must agree that no figure of sufficient insight and political genius appeared on the political scene to lead the way. Of oratory there was no lack. Of determined and wise leadership, all too little.

At the end of the last century there was a lesser, but serious, missed opportunity for Democratic leadership in President Cleveland's failure to grasp the significance of the Populist and labor unrest of the eighties and nineties and in his cautious and unimaginative approach to economic depression. The unrest of these decades did not spring from a radical movement directed against the established order of property or the constitutional system. It grew out of conditions increasingly distressing for the vast majority of the people on the farms and in the factories. Its purposes were the historic purposes of the Democratic party, to safeguard and advance the many interests of many people, to keep opportunity open, opportunity not merely to rise from barefoot boy to President but for people to find in their accustomed environments useful, respected, and satisfying lives. On the farm the closing of the frontier, falling agricultural prices, the growing burden of debt, discriminatory practices by railroads, grain elevators, financial institutions were joining to depress life to the subsistence level and below it. To the factory worker, the movement from country to city, increasing immigration, and the growth of concentration of ownership and size of the industrial unit were having the same effect on wages and working conditions. The conditions and popular response had many points of similarity to those of the 1930's.

Grover Cleveland was a man of honor, courage, and integrity. He followed the right as he saw it. But he saw it through a conservative and conventional cast of mind. The agitation seemed to him, or was made to appear to him, as a threat to law and order. Some, indeed most, of the measures proposed for political reform and fiscal management challenged accepted notions of representative government and what were thought to be the immutable principles which underlay the economic order. So Coxey's Army was met with a barrage of injunctions and finally gathered up by the Capitol police—a rather mild preview of General MacArthur's march down Pennsylvania Avenue in 1932 at the head of his troops to dislodge the unemployed veterans squatting in the condemned and half-destroyed buildings on the south side of the Avenue. The Pullman strike was smashed by Federal troops who kept the mails moving, the union leaders imprisoned, and the union crushed. And the financial panic was dealt with through the highly orthodox and compensated assistance of Mr. Morgan.

The underlying causes of these troubles were neither understood nor dealt with and herein an opportunity was missed which did not recur. If, to take one of them, the problems arising out of the concentration of industrial ownership had been tackled when they were still malleable and subject to effective treatment, we might have been spared some aches and pains which are still with us.

But with all this, Grover Cleveland holds an honored place in the list of the Democratic creators of the unwritten constitution. He rescued the Presidency from two decades of Legislative encroachment on Executive power. He rejected the notion, unhappily recently revived, that the Executive had to get along with Congress, as in progressive education when the child must "integrate himself with the group." He acted on the sound assumption that the constitutional arrangement called for "power as the rival of power." And he did not hesitate to use the veto power—which is equal to two-thirds of the combined strength of Congress—to protect the integrity of his office. Indeed, he was called the Veto President. In foreign affairs, in particular, he reclaimed for the Presidency the right to be the chief organ for the conduct of foreign affairs. When the Congress showed signs of following its own passions to the point of declaring war against Spain, Cleveland put an end to the business for the duration of his administration by saying in effect that, if the Congress did declare war, he would refuse to direct it as Commander in Chief.

The failures in Democratic leadership must be mentioned along with the greater record of distinguished and successful service, so that omission may not distort the story and also because they bring out an essential truth. The Democratic party is made up of people—its members and leaders. It is not a machine operating relentlessly in accordance with mechanical principles. And it makes a world of difference what sort of people its leaders are and what sort of equipment they possess for understanding and leadership. It is true that principles play their important part, but principles exist through men believing and acting. And men act not generally but in concrete situations which they understand always imperfectly. The degree of success in action will be related to the degree of understanding and to the quality of leadership.

3

Modern Democracy—
The Intertwined Strands:
Conservatism and Empiricism

FROM what has been said, it is clear that the Democratic party is not an ideological party. It is not and
cannot be doctrinaire. It represents too many interests
to be neatly labeled or to be imprisoned in the strait
jacket of a formula. It has to be pragmatic. In fact,
neither one of our parties can be truly said to be doctrinaire, but in the battle of dialectics the Republicans
more nearly approach it. As Mr. Harrison hints, they
have not yet wholly realized that for better or for worse
their party "must build on its business base," and in so
far as Republicanism has found articulate and authorita-
tive expression, Mr. Herbert Hoover and Senator Taft
have given it in terms of mid-nineteenth century British
liberalism.

In the Democratic party run two strong strands—conservatism and pragmatic experimentation. This combination is peculiarly American and has been from the earliest days. We cling to the familiar and are always ready to try something new. It can almost be said of us, as an Englishman said of his compatriots, that the best recommendation of an innovation is to call it a revival.

I have suggested that the difference between our parties has not been and is not between a party of property and one of proletarians, but between a party which centers on the dominant interests of the business community and a party of many interests, including property interests. And these property interests run through all the groups which support the Democratic party. They all see their interest and their future within the institution of private property. They believe in private property and want more and not less of it. This makes for conservatism.

American labor is now known throughout the world for its conservatism. Property holdings in all forms by labor organizations and individuals are most substantial. One of the most consistent efforts of labor policy has been to transpose some of the attributes of property into the tenure of the job. The whole stress on seniority grows out of this. Pension rights are property interests of impressive value. Labor finds a sympathetic hearing and response in the Democratic party and has important interests to protect and advance through governmental action. But labor also has interests which it guards as jealously against governmental interference as does business itself—the running of its own affairs, the making of its own bargains, the right to strike. Nationalization of industry finds no echo in American labor. In the railroad brotherhoods the Plumb Plan of the early nineteen-twenties has left no trace.

Again, when a particular kind of property descends in the hierarchy of importance, its owners more and more turn for the protection of their interests to the party of many interests. The owners of land—the farmers—are the most crucial of these groups. When the majority of them vote with the Democratic party, it wins; and, when they do not, it loses. Small businessmen, also, are apt to find concern for their problems and welfare lost in the party of business on a larger scale. These groups, too, make for conservatism.

But perhaps the strongest influence toward conservatism comes from the South, where for historical reasons all interests, business and otherwise, are predominantly Democratic. The most conservative leaders in the party come from the South. This sometimes causes impatience among Northern liberals. But Southern conservatism is an invaluable asset. It gives the assurance that all interests and policies are weighed and considered within the party before interparty issues are framed. There can be no greater deterrent to the forcing of extremes and the creation of class parties. It does not seem extravagant to say that the Democratic party is one of the strongest cohesive factors in American life, holding together and reconciling, as it does, sectional and economic interests.

The South also faces us with an equal and opposite truth. It is that some of the most radical leaders of modern times have also come from the South. We tend to see men like Watson, Tillman, Vardaman, and Huey Long chiefly in terms of their bellowings about White Supremacy. But if we drain this off—and the *if* is admittedly of major importance—what we should see is that the mass support of these men was formed by the dispossessed. Huey Long's "share-the-wealth" program was aimed explicitly at the Southern Bourbons, as was the Populist drive headed by Watson. The tragedy of the South has been that racism has corrupted an otherwise respectable strain of protest and experimentation in the search for economic equality, dating back to Jefferson, Mason, Randolph, and Jackson. For all the apparent contradiction in the fact that the Southern racist belongs to the same political party as the New York supporter of the FEPC,[1] the inner logic which holds them together is that each speaks for the dispossessed, whether in his rural or urban form. What enables the Democratic party to contain both elements is the fact that the party since

[1] Fair Employment Practice Committee.

the Civil War has made the Legislature the special province of the Southern Democrat, and the Executive the special province of the Northern Democrat. One wing therefore is in a position to check the other within government proper, while each vis-à-vis the other, is compelled to give a little and take a little until some sort of consensus is reached.

Entwined with the strand of conservatism in the Democratic party is the strand of empiricism. A party which represents many interests and is composed of many diverse groups must inevitably know that human institutions are made for man and not man for institutions. Rules and formulae are not and cannot be permitted to be sovereign. "To rest upon a formula is a slumber that, prolonged, means death."[2] Such a party conceives of government as an instrument to accomplish what needs to be done, even if this cuts across cherished doctrines, as the Louisiana Purchase cut across narrow construction of granted powers under the Constitution. And once government is thought of as an instrument which can affect the outcome of events, this leads to a greater willingness to experiment, to check by regulation actions thought to be undesirable, and to stimulate desired developments which seem to be lagging—the Securities and Exchange Act and the Public Utility Holding Com-

[2] Oliver Wendell Holmes, "Ideals and Doubts," *Collected Legal Papers* (Harcourt, Brace and Company, New York, 1920), pp. 303, 306.

pany Act on one side, the Tennessee Valley Authority
Act on the other.

This is not so easy for those who are persuaded that
human behavior is governed by immutable laws, whether
they are the laws expounded in the *Social Statics* of Herbert Spencer or those in *Das Kapital* of Karl Marx.
Stalin tried to get around this impediment by stating
that, while economic laws were absolute, those who
understood them could put them to use as engineers put
to use the laws of physics in damming a river. But to the
Manchester Liberals the Factory Acts ran squarely
counter to economic principles and could end only in
disaster. The "forgotten man," in the phrase invented
by William Graham Sumner, was not the man meant
in our day when the phrase was revived. He was the pro-
ducer whose wealth was tapped by the government to
bear the cost of social programs for those whom Sumner
regarded as the weaklings, the casualties of the industrial
process. The majority reports of the second Hoover
Commission retain the same image.

In the last century the economically powerful have
stood to gain by the doctrine of laissez faire and the idea
that governmental or other interference with "natural"
economic laws was both futile and evil. It was those
whose interests were suffering under the impact of new
forces who looked to government to be something more
than policeman, judge, and soldier. They saw the neces-

sity for some managerial power to be added—not to control and direct all activity, but to manage the thrust of forces in the interest of human values.

Now to carry out a function of this sort requires knowledge, perceptiveness, imagination—in other words, brains. Generally speaking, a policy of doing as little as possible requires less brains than one of anticipating trouble and of doing whatever is necessary. So the Democratic party is hospitable to and attracts intellectuals. It has work for them to do. In the last twenty years it had a vast amount of work for them to do. And the enduring quality of what they did bears testimony that it was well done.

The Republican party is cool to intellectuals, unless they are lawyers, when they talk about government. They are apt to be called "eggheads," "radicals," or "pinkos," for their pains. In industry intellectuals are likely to be found in the laboratory or designing room, or on the construction job, or in the operating plant. Before they are welcomed into the ranks of those who formulate high policy, "practical" experience has usually tempered their "theoretical" approach. So the Democratic party, strange as it might have seemed to Old Hickory but not to Mr. Jefferson, Mr. Wilson, or Mr. Roosevelt, is the party which attracts intellectuals and puts them to work.

The effect of the combination of conservatism and empiricism of which I have spoken is nowhere better shown than in the actions taken by the New Deal of President Roosevelt to meet the great depression. The failure of President Hoover had not been due to lack of understanding of the facts of the depression or of sympathy with its victims. It was a failure of leadership and lack of willingness to use the powers of government to do what could not be done by any other power. Government, as Mr. Hoover saw it, had a limited function, which became a wholly inadequate one as the disaster grew. The government in Washington should plan, advise, exhort, and encourage business and local government. But it should not act, direct, or order. It would be wrong for it to throw its own credit and resources into the gap left by the collapse of private, state, and municipal credit. The federal government had no responsibility and no proper authority to reactivate finance and industry or to deal with relief. To the millions who were suffering physical privation and the loss of their farms, homes, businesses, jobs, bank accounts, and investments this attitude seemed callous and defeatist.

The New Deal was under no such self-imposed limitation. After the new President had said in his inaugural address that the only thing we had to fear was fear itself, he proceeded to act on every front with imagination, vigor, and courage. He conceived of the federal government as the whole people organized to do what had to be done, and he galvanized its will to action. Not all that was done appears wholly wise in retrospect. The National Recovery Administration, for instance, got itself into a series of dead-end efforts from which it was rescued only by its demise. But the impact of spirited attack along the whole wide front was profoundly effective. It not only produced economic results but spiritual results of great importance. The people were no longer called upon to bear their fate with courageous resignation and to learn patiently the lessons which it taught. They had a leader who told them that by their own organized effort they could end their miseries and they had a government which would lead the way and mobilize the means.

All the problems were attacked at once. Government credit was put behind the saving of homes and farms and the reopening of banks. Work programs were financed to provide relief and new purchasing power for business. Municipal, state, and federal public works stimulated the building and heavy industries. Agricultural production and prices were taken in hand by the Agricultural Adjustment Administration and industrial production by the National Recovery Administration. A road into future development was opened by the public power program to expand the fundamental requisite of an industrial civilization—energy. Housing projects, new labor legislation, the social security enactments, the school and youth programs carried the promise that recovery would also be progress throughout the population.

It is not my purpose to write a history or eulogy of the New Deal's recovery legislation, but to recall its breadth, imagination, and vigor, its basic attitude toward the function and responsibility of government. And I wish to recall something else—its essential conservatism. Its purpose and effect was to bring to new life and strength, to even wider acceptance and participation, the system of private ownership of property.

The New Deal did not turn to a system of collective farming, nor did it result in a vast increase in farmlands owned by mortgagors, the insurance companies and banks. It saved individual ownership by individual farmers and increased it. There was no nationalization of banks and industries.

During the talk with my client which I mentioned earlier, he freely agreed that after fifteen years of Democratic control in Washington his own business was larger, stronger, more virile and independent, more confident of its future than it had ever been. He complained of taxes and unorthodox finance and the antitrust laws, but he did not believe anyone had attempted to socialize him. Even the activities of Washington in the field of relief, which had seemed to him to contain threats to the balance of our federal system, had pretty well disappeared along with the need which inspired them.

Nor was my friend the only magnate to whom many of the New Deal measures—so long as they were not

identified as such—had become proper parts of an
accepted scheme of things. During the study of the stock
market in the spring of 1955 by the Senate Banking and
Currency Committee, headed by Senator Fulbright,
one witness after another from industry and finance
argued that the market was strong and immune from collapse on the 1929 style. Why? Because, so they said, of
legislation which had removed the abuses of the 1920's,
provided safety mechanisms, and redistributed purchasing power. What they were talking about was New Deal
legislation—which most of them had fought with tenac-
ity, but now praised without identifying it by name and
origin.

If we take public power itself, we see now how basi-
cally conservative the Tennessee Valley Authority, for instance, was and is. Far from being creeping socialism, it
is more nearly an instrument of galloping capitalism.
There is more property, more privately owned property,
and more value in that property, in the Tennessee Valley
today than there ever was before. And it has increased
more rapidly than in other parts of the country. There is
more business, more private initiative, and more independence and rampant individualism. And why not?
Without electrical energy the region was doomed to
backwardness and comparative poverty, just as it would
have been without roads. The TVA provided that energy

when others could not, and the energy stimulated the productivity to pay for it.

President Hoover thought otherwise. On March 3, 1931, he vetoed the Muscle Shoals bill, the predecessor of TVA. I quote a portion of his veto message since it quite transcends my capacity—and indeed the reader's tolerance of any such attempt by me—to state the Republican point of view.

But for the Federal Government deliberately to go out to build up and expand such an occasion [flood control] to the major purpose of a power and manufacturing business is to break down the initiative and enterprise of the American people; it is destruction of equality of opportunity amongst our people; it is the negation of the ideals upon which our civilization has been based.

. . . I hesitate to contemplate the future of our institutions, of our Government, and of our country if the preoccupation of its officials is to be no longer the promotion of justice and equal opportunity but is to be devoted to barter in the markets. That is not liberalism, it is degeneration.[3]

Now, almost a quarter of a century later, the second Hoover Commission reiterates the same views,[4] demonstrating their imperviousness to time and experience.

Not to prolong or overwork illustration, I think it fair

[3] *Congressional Record*, Vol. 74, Part 7 (March 3, 1931), pp. 7047-7048.
[4] Commission on Organization of the Executive Branch of the Government, *Water Resources and Power*, June, 1955.

to say that by and large the New Deal was a clinic in the use of innovation to conserve and strengthen fundamental institutions. The subsequent history of its principal measures, I believe, shows that this is true. Despite years of vitriolic attack on the New Deal and its principal figures and an overturn in political control, its measures survive, indeed have been accepted as part of the permanent laws of the land.

Social security and the interest of the federal government in education and welfare have been thought important enough by the Republican Administration to be entrusted to a new department of government. With the exception of the Taft-Hartley amendments to the Wagner Act, a whole code of laws relating to labor-management relations and fair labor standards remain upon the books. The same is true in agriculture, hardly any part of which is unaffected—production and marketing, price support, farm and home credit, soil conservation, commodity exchange regulation, crop insurance. It all remains. No one suggests changes in the banking or gold legislation, the regulation of the exchanges or utility holding companies. Those who are restive under the legislative policies on public power and conservation of natural resources will not risk a frontal attack on these but turn to administrative nibbling away.

And so it goes. The new, the unfamiliar, the highly controversial measures of yesterday have become familiar and respectable. They have joined the Interstate Commerce Act, the Granger legislation, the Antitrust Acts, and the Federal Reserve Act in the Pantheon of legislation.

Let me say again that I do not wish to cast a rosy light over all that was done or proposed. Some mistaken features of the National Recovery Administration have already been mentioned. In one case, at least, a harsher judgment must be given—the Supreme Court proposals of 1937. These were ill-conceived and wrong. They belong with earlier agitation for the recall of judges and the recall of judicial decisions. Perhaps they were worse, since they were not so frank; and more unwise, because they were unnecessary. But we should not be sanctimonious about the matter and fail to recall that there was much provocation. Justice Holmes stated it when this century was young: "When twenty years ago a vague terror went over the earth and the word socialism began to be heard, I thought and still think that fear was translated into doctrines that had no proper place in the Constitution or the common law."[5]

Years later Woodrow Wilson echoed this concern: "The most obvious and immediate danger to which we are exposed is that the courts will more and more outrage the common people's sense of justice and cause a revulsion against judicial authority which may seriously

[5] Oliver Wendell Holmes, "Law and the Court," op. cit., pp. 291, 295.

disturb the equilibrium of our institutions, and I see nothing which can save us from this danger if the Supreme Court is to repudiate liberal courses of thought and action."[6]

The decisions to which the Justice and the former President referred were placing anachronistic blocks in the path of legislation familiar and necessary in all modern states to meet the growing problems of industrialization—the control of child labor, of hours of labor and minimum wages for women, the regulation of businesses which affected the public interest, and so on. But the education of a new generation of lawyers and judges and the effects of time upon the older generation were bound to bring a change. They did so swiftly on the Supreme Court. From 1937 to 1940 five justices were replaced by new appointees and in 1941 two more. Even as the President bent his bow for what became known as "the Supreme Court fight," the real problem was on the eve of disappearance. But the *Schechter* case,[7] then known as the sick-chicken case, aroused in the Administration all the emotions of a disappointed litigant, which are always poignant, and led it to confuse a well-deserved check upon administrative law with the more justified impatience over outgrown concepts.

The shaft was loosed, a tragic mistake, and for the

[6] Letter to Mr. Justice John H. Clarke, September, 1922, *Woodrow Wilson; Life and Letters*, R. S. Baker (Doubleday, Page & Co., Garden City, N.Y., 1927-39), Vol. 6, p. 117.

[7] *Schechter Poultry Corp.* v. *United States*, 295 U.S. 495 (1935).

greater part of 1937 the country was thrown into alarmed and outraged turmoil. The attack on the Court failed, but much harm was done, both to the Court and to the Administration. We may say of this battle, as we shall have occasion to say of the attack on government itself thirteen years later—again in the words of Justice Holmes—"When the ignorant are taught to doubt they do not know what they safely may believe."[8] The significance of the episode here is that it obscured for years what has been stressed here, the underlying conservatism of the innovations of the New Deal.

One final observation seems pertinent on this part of our discussion. A danger which is always run in the administration of policies—I have often seen it in foreign policy—is that means tend to become confused with ends. A particular program or measure tends to become identified with the policy which it is intended to further. Programs are always easier to identify and support than the broader and more distant purposes which they serve. This is a special danger for a party which is empirical in its methods, since it leads to rigidity of attitude. It leads to a clinging to programs or measures for their own sake after they have served their purpose, to the establishment of a new vested interest in the *status quo*. Empiricism has got to remain empirical. It ceases to be

[8] Oliver Wendell Holmes, "Law and the Court," *op. cit.*, pp. 291, 292.

if, for instance, the worth of public housing becomes a dogma which obstructs a continually fresh examination of whether it remains a needed and sound means of furnishing adequate housing for the American people. Similarly, fixed parity prices for agricultural commodities may have moved from a useful expedient to meet an acute problem on a temporary basis to a policy in its own right. Whether this is so or not, the way to find out is to subject the program to continual pragmatic examination in the light of the objective sought—a workable policy for the furtherance of American agriculture which is compatible with other American interests. All must make some sacrifices in the common interest; none are entitled to a preferred position; and all deserve effective support when in real trouble. The mutual criticism of a many-interest party is a good method of achieving this. Fixed prices and government purchase of surpluses is probably not a principle for general application to lawyers, automobile workers, and others. Perhaps there are special reasons for continuing it in agriculture. If so, where do we end up? I do not know the answers and do not mean to discuss the question. I stress only that, if we abandon pragmatic analysis and candid mutual criticism, we shall abandon something pretty basic in the Democratic party.

These and other criticisms and warnings can be voiced on what was done. But they do not weaken or obscure the central point. Modern democracy has shown amazing vitality and imagination in innovation which has conserved and strengthened the fundamental institutions of our American life. So soundly has it worked that what was once novel and controversial is now accepted as a matter of course by former friend and foe alike.

4

Modern Democracy

in Foreign Affairs

1. HISTORY HAS SHAPED BROAD PARTY ATTITUDES.

It is always dangerous to attribute principles, behavior, or attitudes to men or institutions on the basis of supposed fundamental characteristics. When I am told that Americans are idealistic and naïve, or that Frenchmen are logical, or Germans emotionally unstable, or Asians devious and inscrutable, I always listen to the ensuing observation with skepticism. Not that such generalizations may not have some basis in fact, but they can rarely carry the superstructure erected on them. Lawyers have a special facility for providing plausible but, in the light of historical scholarship, wholly incorrect explanations for legal rules. So I shall both bridle myself and warn the reader that it is most unsafe to find reasons for the attitudes of our political parties on foreign affairs in the composition and basis of the parties themselves.

I suppose that during most of the nineteenth century almost all Americans were hemispheric isolationists. There was really no other choice, just as it has been said that in England all classes were conservative until under the Tudors the Reformation presented a choice between the old and the new which could not be avoided. Certainly from the winning of independence to near the close of the nineteenth century, the chief bent of our diplomacy was directed to the acquisition of land on the North American mainland, and to the prevention of European sovereignties doing so within the hemisphere. Foreign affairs became almost a branch of domestic policy as we adventured on our ocean-to-ocean march, sought the outer limits of our territory to the north and south, with each new acquisition of land threatening to upset the balance of political, social, and economic forces within the nation. Not that we divorced ourselves from world affairs. Indeed, we played off the great powers one against the other—England, France, and Spain, plus the shadowy power of the Indian tribes. And among these, we picked our enemies and friends by the measure and the importance of the land they held or could help us get on or near the American continent. It was Jefferson who wrote, "There is on the globe one single spot, the possessor of which is our natural and habitual enemy.

... From that moment [the day of French possession of New Orleans] we must marry ourselves to the British fleet and nation . . . [to hold] the two continents of America in sequestration for the common purposes of the united British and American nations."[1]

Toward the close of the nineteenth century and the beginning of the twentieth, the center of American action moved from a continental to an oceanic diplomacy, seen not only in the war with Spain, but in our intervention in the course of the Russo-Japanese War. Now, more and more, the old aim of land, specific and measurable, was displaced by the intangible but nevertheless real aim expressed in terms of interests —strategic, economic, political, and cultural. Now, too, we had to give thought not to short-run relations limited to the length of a war and involving only two or three nations, but to longer relationships having no terminal date with groups of nations themselves interrelated. But as yet the realization of this changed situation had no wide acceptance among our people.

The First World War brought us Americans face to face with this reality and with some others. It also faced us with the necessity of making a choice in our foreign relations. The matrix of our isolation from the conflicts and struggles of the European nations was gone, and

[1] Letter to Robert R. Livingston, April 18, 1802, *The Writings of Thomas Jefferson* (G. P. Putnam's Sons, Ford Ed., New York, 1892-99), Vol. VIII, pp. 143, 144-145.

with it, our remoteness and the security which came from it. The British sea power which furnished the original sanction behind the Monroe Doctrine and had contributed to the realization of our desire to enjoy peace and prosperity undisturbed—a desire entirely consistent with British interests—was no longer supreme and unchallenged in the Atlantic. On the contrary, by 1917 British sea power had been unable to hold the seas against German submarine attack. Within two years the Atlantic had changed for us from a vast protective moat to an undefended plain reaching to our very shores and threatened with the domination of a hostile power. The United States of necessity entered the war to protect itself, and restored the balance of power in its own interest.

From then on the choices presented to us were unavoidable. What was not sufficiently clear to enough Americans was what the choices were and which was right. One choice was for us to continue purposefully to affect international affairs so as to maintain an environment favorable to our interests—an environment in which nations seeking peace and individual freedom might flourish. This choice required continuous, vigorous, and responsible American participation in international affairs. In and out participation would not do. As Mr. A. J. P. Taylor has so graphically pointed out,[2] even before the First World War one gifted with rare perception might have seen that a balance of power capable of maintaining peace was no longer possible among only European nations. In the hundred years following the Congress of Vienna the center of power in Europe moved eastward, and the combinations to balance the strongest shifted and became less capable of doing so. In 1815 all of Europe was required to equal the power of France. Later the power of the Holy Alliance—Russia, Austria, and Prussia—was matched by Britain and Western Europe. As Germany came into existence and joined scientific and technical skill with population and resources, the power of Russia had to be shifted to the Triple Entente, and even then it was inadequate without America. Today, as the Soviet Union repeats the experience in technology and outstrips it in resources and population, it is plain that no security is possible without America in the balancing system and that no security for America is possible without such a system.

The other choice was again to withdraw from world affairs. To some this choice appealed because they misread the significance and consequences of German defeat. They believed that this meant that we could not again be menaced from without. Or, if we should be

[2] *The Struggle for Mastery in Europe, 1848-1918* (Oxford University Press, London, 1954).

again threatened, others thought that the menace should be combatted from Fortress America rather than in an association with other nations, which had proved very disillusioning to them. The realities of international life were disturbing and shocking to many who had taken a romantic view of the war and of America's mission in it.

Again, after the Second World War these choices were presented, but with less question in our minds about which was the right choice. They still remain the choices today.

In considering the attitude of the two political parties toward these choices, one fact seems to me pre-eminent. In both of the two great fluid periods of the twentieth century—the periods just before, during, and after the two World Wars—the Democrats were in the position of responsibility for the conduct of foreign affairs, while the Republicans were in opposition and without executive responsibility. This, I think, had more to do with the hardening of attitudes than innate party characteristics. The Democratic attitude was formed by a government in power, responsible for its acts, and with that intimate knowledge of the new pressures and necessities which comes only from the conduct of affairs. The Republicans, quite naturally, were seeking political leverage with which to obtain power. Their interest turned inward to the domestic political scene where the forces which could be exploited were the reaction from the burdens and discipline of war and the reluctance to assume heavy and altogether novel commitments and responsibilities far beyond our shores and our experience. The outside world, as it actually existed, was grim and forbidding with heavy burdens and responsibilities attached to power. On the other side, contrasting with it, was the memory of the world as it had been and as one wished that it might be. Between must lie error and fault. Someone must be to blame for this discrepancy between what was and what ought to be after such vast effort.

In 1919-20 the attack on the Democrats was savage and malicious. In 1950-52 the ferocity of the Republican attack knew no limits. It went beyond the policies involved and the competence of leaders. It struck at the character and patriotism of those who devised and executed policies. It assaulted institutions of government and, as in the Bricker Amendment, even government itself. Nor did it stop at the water's edge. It involved the motives and character of nations and peoples associated with us. It is hardly too much to say that the whole conception of trust and confidence, including the confidence of the people in their own judgment, was brought into doubt. Officials and departments of government, the army, civil servants, a whole political party, the labor movement, teachers and institutions, churches, writers and artists, all were cast into the limbo of doubt.

The house of government was gutted. The new tenants found themselves the inheritors of suspicion. For, as we said before, "when the ignorant are taught to doubt they do not know what they safely may believe."

From these historical experiences come, I think, the major influences in the formation of political attitudes toward foreign affairs—the Democrats acutely conscious that we live in a world that has cut deeply into our lives and fortunes and can do so again; the Republicans acutely conscious of the domestic forces which they have twice used to overthrow their opponents.

These two influences have produced another fact important in understanding the conduct of the parties in foreign affairs. It is that the Democrats are now pretty well united in their attitude; the Republicans pretty well divided in theirs. For during and after the Second World War, the prior Republican attitude of isolationism became so divorced from the realities of the world as it was that many Republicans turned away from it. The split went deep and became reflected in the rival candidates for the Presidential nomination in 1952. General Eisenhower's victory was not achieved without inflicting wounds that are still unhealed. The dissident faction of the party is compact, articulate, and often ruthless. In the Senate, for instance, this wing of the party is probably the stronger. It certainly is on matters of economic foreign policy, as the experience of the Randall Commission and the party divisions over the Reciprocal Trade Agreements Act demonstrated.

The fact of a divided party has in itself far-reaching consequences. Foreign policy today is not a matter, as it once was, merely of declarations by the Executive, even of such important declarations as the Monroe Doctrine. It involves sustained and costly programs, like the Greek-Turkish Program, the Marshall Plan, NATO, the Voice of America, the Military Assistance Program, and the building up of our defense—to name only a few. And these in turn require continuity of legislation and provision of funds. Basic also in our modern foreign policy is the confidence of our allies in the steadiness of our actions and behavior generally.

It is hard to meet these necessities when a divided Republican party results, as it must, in a multiplicity of voices, in a course of starts and stops, turns and twists, as the leader in the White House and his lieutenants in the State Department angle for the support of their own party with a series of compromises. American politics are in an odd state when the Administration in power is furnished respite and support only by losing control of the Congress to the Democrats.

So much for the effect of past experience upon party attitudes toward foreign affairs.

2. ENTER THE ATOM—THE HAZARD WHICH RIDES UPON
   CHANCE OR ERROR.

The discoveries of the nuclear physicists have given
to the conduct of foreign relations a somberness and
hazard which neither domestic nor international politics
has ever held before. Both at home and abroad there
hangs over all of us the brooding omnipresent possibility
that if things go wrong enough in our foreign relations a
vast number of us here and elsewhere may be blown to
bits and with us a good many of our cities and the industries which support our national lives. Even the
nation-states of which we are citizens may not continue
in anything like the form in which we now know them.

This is the hazard which rides upon chance or error.
This is what gives a tenseness and solemnity to the moves
which our statesmen make for us. This is what underlies
the necessity for thought, hard thought, and plenty of
it, as nothing ever did before.

There is an odd pastime, which we occasionally read
about in the newspapers, called Russian roulette. One
puts a single cartridge in a revolver, spins the chamber,
then puts the muzzle against one's head and pulls the
trigger. If only a click results, one passes the revolver to
the next player, who repeats the process. Sooner or later
something more than a click results.

It is moderate to say that in this game the hazard

risked upon chance is excessive. In our foreign affairs
such risks are possible, too. It is unwise to take them.
The very existence of these risks today is one of the
postulates which must enter into and profoundly affect
what we do and don't do abroad. Most of us dislike
thinking about atomic and hydrogen bombs. It is all so
secret, so far beyond our grasp that we feel helpless and
fatalistic and want to put it all out of our minds. But
we had better take a look at some of the implications
and perhaps we can have some thoughts that are not
altogether useless.

In the first place we can take it to be true that at
present the Soviet Union and we could each inflict disastrous devastation on the other. The first attack,
if it were a surprise, could be the more damaging; but
the counterattack could be bad enough. Neither of us
could prevent the damage, though each might through
defensive systems substantially reduce the full potential.
As the destructive power of the bombs increases, the
defense becomes less effective, since each one that gets
through can do more harm. It is probable that this situation will continue. It is possible that in this situation our
position will become more disadvantageous for us unless
the extent of our effort is increased.

Everything that I have said can be disputed by the
experts and the military men, and infinite qualifications
and refinements added. But I think for our purposes it

is a true starting point. I have heard the claims of the scientists and of the military men a good many times and respect their justifiable pride in their services. It can be argued, for instance, that nuclear weapons can be developed for precision bombing—say, to destroy the opposing air force and nuclear establishments—and that self-interest through the fear of retaliation will prevent their use on population centers. It can be argued that the defense, now behind the offense in development, may be brought abreast of it. All these possibilities exist, but human error and miscalculations will always exist, too. To rely on the optimum in making a policy is to play Russian roulette. So we start from the premise that with atomic warfare very great mutual destruction is probable. After the first exchange of blows others are likely, but it is not necessary to pursue these into doubtful prophecy.

I think it should also be assumed that, if hostilities (I am not referring to isolated patrol or air clashes) should start in Europe or elsewhere, which engaged our own and Soviet forces, atomic attacks on continental United States must be expected. This seems the only safe assumption, both because of the desire of the other side to strike a crippling blow at the center of the opposed military and industrial strength, and also because, if tactical weapons are used, there will be strong pressures to widen the area of attack and counterattack until it ends in strategic bombing. I see no line short of it which under the pressures of war the self-interest of both sides is likely to draw and to maintain.

The conclusion I reach is that war between the Soviet Union and the United States would in all probability bring such devastation and carnage to the two participants, and to other countries as well, that it should be a major purpose of our foreign policy (and theirs as well) to avoid it. By a major purpose I mean one in the very highest category of objectives to be sought and achieved. The possibility of atomic war must be squarely faced and prepared for, since it is plain that if one party in the last analysis is willing to fight and the other is not, the will of the former will prevail. But so long as rationality controls conduct on both sides, it should be, and I think will be, directed to avoiding nuclear war and acts that lead to such a war.

The risk is that those in control may not act rationally or may miscalculate; that they may start and keep in motion a train of events under a misapprehension of its results, or the reaction to it, until the point of no return has been passed. Irrational persons have reached positions of decisive power before. Hitler was such a person. There can be others like him. No precaution can assure against this. It is a risk which must be borne, like the risk of drunken men driving automobiles. The risks of miscalculation can be reduced by learning how to calculate and by always being responsible about it. But these risks, too, cannot be eliminated. They have to be borne.

The result is that we live always in imminent danger. This is a hard position for everyone. It is particularly hard for us, because it is so new to us. Many of us cannot tolerate the anxiety of insecurity and must find an end to it. Two ends suggest themselves. One is to rush into the disaster and have it over with. The other is to remove the instrumentality of such vast destructive power—the atomic and hydrogen weapon—by various devices of international agreement.

To advocate having it over with, ending the anxiety by precipitating atomic war, shows, I think, that to reason from dubious premises can present dangers as great as not to reason at all. For logic is no better and can be no more certain than its premises. I doubt whether any man can see into the future far enough or clearly enough to warrant destroying so many and so much upon the probability that what he sees will in fact come to pass. And what is it that he seems to see? Future developments by which the damage that can be done to us increases both absolutely and in proportion to what we can inflict, until, not only does the outcome of the struggle become doubtful, but the question arises whether we should survive it at all. Nor is this all. He sees, too, as these disadvantageous changes occur, an increased willingness on the part of those who can do so to attack us.

Why, he asks, wait for this disaster? The thinker I am imagining would not do so. He would anticipate the fulfillment of his prophecy by acts, the consequences of which also lie in the realm of prophecy. He would argue, I assume, that our preventive attack would prevent any retaliation against us by destroying the other side's capacity to retaliate—its air force and bombs. But, here, as has been pointed out, he is playing Russian roulette. Any plan based on such an expectation simply cannot be adopted by sensible men—to say nothing of moral men. We must for purposes of policy planning accept the high probability that a preventive attack would not prevent retaliation. It would bring it about.

What would happen then? Would our people dig themselves out of the rubble and wreck of their houses and cities and fight a long war to victory? Would the response be the response to Pearl Harbor? Perhaps. But Pearl Harbor was a sneak attack on us, not retaliation for a sneak attack by us. And what would be the attitude of the other peoples of the world who found that world tumbling about their ears because we had had a nightmare? Isn't it possible that all of them, our own people and the others, too, would have strong views about those leaders who had brought all this on without their consent? This consent clearly could not be asked and given, since to do so would precipitate the blow which by hypothesis our thinker wants to anticipate.

But there are still deeper obscurities attached to "having it over with." The one thing which we can be sure of in this uncertain world is that the consequences of letting loose unlimited force are unpredictable. No one in 1914 or 1939 had the remotest idea that the outcomes would be what they were. So we can write it down as certain that whatever might eventuate for us as a result of precipitating atomic war would be different from any expectation and could well be infinitely worse. The reasoning which is relied on to support this course is based upon premises about dangers and consequences which are far too fragile and speculative to support the awful weight of the conclusion drawn. It is rather a nostalgic urge to find once again the security which we have lost forever, but which, failing to find it, is transformed into an impulse to embrace disaster in order to escape anxiety.

Some pages above I mentioned another course which suggests itself to those seeking an end to the insecurity and anxiety bred of nuclear armaments. This course was to abolish nuclear armaments—and anxiety with them—through some device of international agreement. Here, I think, we should have our minds quite clear that, great as would be the consequent *reduction* in anxiety, the danger of nuclear destruction will always remain so long as there remains the danger of war between nations capable of producing nuclear weapons. For war means the breakdown of all restraints on the use of force between the belligerents, except those dictated by self-interest. Even though nuclear armaments might not be in existence at the beginning of a war—as they were not at the beginning of World War II—they would be at its end—and probably in connection with its end.

I say this not to deprecate the efforts of our government, during the last Administration and the present one, to bring atomic energy under international control, and other armaments likewise. If these could be carried to success, which the attitude of the Soviet government makes doubtful, the anxiety would no longer be that of sitting on a powder keg with lighted matches. This would be a great achievement. But it brings us face to face with the basic hazard of our time. This is that some nation-states know how to blow each other and others apart and will in all probability do so if things go badly enough between them.

If this is so, it must, I suggest, profoundly change our attitude toward major war as an element in the grand strategy of our relations with the rest of the nation-states which make up our world. Much as we may dislike the thought, most wars which our nation has fought throughout its history have been regarded by contemporary Americans as means of accomplishing national purposes beyond overcoming the armed force of an enemy, even though they have simultaneously experienced all the humane emotions of abhorrence of war. I am not suggesting that they instigated or chose this method and that the wars were not forced upon them. That is aside from my point, which is that, however they came, most of these wars were regarded as, and indeed were, means—detested and deplored, but nevertheless means—by which some desired end could be achieved when the resort to force had ended. Although it would never have been put in the language of Clausewitz, war was a continuation of political intercourse with an admixture of other means.

Our attitude contemplated objectives of a larger nature than the successful conduct of war alone. After force met and overcame the force of the enemy, it was contemplated that other means would take over to achieve the end desired. The end might be a simple one, to acquire territory or to eject another power from specific territory, or it might be more complex, or even unformulated, like gaining control of the seas, or readjusting the balance of power, or establishing a more secure environment for our free system of life. Even in those instances where the national purpose was to meet and defeat force applied against us, this, too, contemplated something beyond the fighting, the resumption of pursuit of ends which the use of force had interrupted.

Many of our disappointments came from a failure to see that war, the use of force itself, could not accomplish these greater purposes of the grand strategy. Force can only overcome other force. When it has done this, it has spent itself and other means of influencing conduct have to be employed. These other methods are difficult and complicated, so much so that we often become impatient and frustrated and complain that our statesmen lose at the conference table what our soldiers have won on the battlefield, as though it were the same thing. What our soldiers have won is the defeat of the enemy's force. What our statesmen are seeking is to further the achievement of ends which the enemy's resort to force interdicted, at least in part.

One of the great delusions, so current in our times, is that victory in war puts the victorious powers in a position in which all they need to do is pick up the spoils of war in the form of their postwar objectives. Victory in war opens this treasure chest; and nothing remains for the victors to do but stuff their pockets. In other words, the postwar objectives have been won by the achievement of victory. At this point of victory, for this moment, the victors seem to enjoy a godlike omnipotence. They can have anything they want. Holding vanquished nations in their power, they can eliminate them from the earth, or make them peace-loving and democratic, or set whatever limits to their policy in perpetuity the victors deem desirable. Millions of men have died for that moment when all things seem possible. But all things are not possible. The moment passes. Force has achieved its limit, and the infinitely difficult processes of obtaining consent, even the consent of the vanquished, for objectives beyond the reach of force have begun. As the politicians and diplomats begin to meet and discuss, it seems to many that those who gave their lives have been betrayed.

Then we begin to learn, too, that war can be conducted in such a way as to make the achievement of desired results thereafter infinitely more difficult. The use of absolute force, unlimited violence, may produce results which themselves defeat the purpose which lies beyond victory over the force opposed to us. There may, of course, be no choice in a struggle for survival. But so long as there remains any choice it is well to remember that unlimited violence and unlimited purposes are very dangerous. One may ask now—though I think the answer is by no means clear—whether "unconditional surrender" as our objective in the last war was wise. One may destroy so much which will be needed later that ends once attainable after victory are no longer within our power.

It is with these thoughts that we should turn to our attitude toward atomic war as an element in the grand strategy of our relations with the rest of the world. We must regard it, I think, as the ultimate in violence, which will be applied to all involved and many who can see no reason to be. It is not force applied against force. It is force applied to whole peoples and their environment. It does not leave a nation with its forces overthrown and amenable to the processes of political intercourse. It leaves devastation everywhere amidst which no policy of peaceful intercourse is now conceivable. It is not an instrument of policy. It is the negation of plan and purpose beyond itself.

So I think atomic war has no positive place as an element of policy. It must be reserved as a weapon in a desperate death struggle forced upon us by an attack on ourselves or a nation so close to us through commitment or interest that the attack is a plain prelude to general conflict. Except in these circumstances we cannot employ it, nor should we threaten to employ it. Vague phrases which suggest we might respond to any less vital danger by atomic retaliation carry the most vicious risk, whether believed or not believed, and may cause a fatal miscalculation. There can be no bluff here. The risks are too great for anything but the most sober and blunt truth. Nothing, I think, would clear the air more than having this understood at home and abroad.

If, then, one of the highest objectives of our foreign policy, of our dealings with the other nation-states which compose our world, is to avoid and prevent war which may develop into nuclear warfare, how do we go about it? In the next chapter we shall see that there are many complex and difficult courses which are both open to us and required of us. Here let us limit ourselves to a narrower question. What is it which foreign policy needs from military policy to aid in working through the present situation as it is and keeping to the minimum the chance of nuclear warfare?

What is needed, I believe, is capacity in three areas:

1. Striking power with nuclear weapons great enough to deter the use of such weapons against us and our friends.

2. The development, with the greatest energy and inventiveness, of defense against such attacks. However difficult it may appear, success comes only to those who labor mightily.

3. A military establishment capable of meeting—we would hope jointly with our friends—force which might be employed against our interests, without involving the world in nuclear warfare.

It should be quite clear that this means the possibility of the limited use of force for the limited purpose of overcoming force which has been used against our interests. To many this seems an unfamiliar and wrong idea. It did not seem so to the Europeans of the later half of the seventeenth century and the eighteenth century up to the French Revolution. They had before them the lessons of the religious wars with their unlimited use of force for unlimited objectives; and they knew its mutually destructive results. If they did not attain an enforced peace, they were careful not to let the use of force get out of control.

Recently a soldier of note stated the opposing view:

Once our leaders, our authorized leaders, the President and Congress, decide that fight we must, in my opinion we should fight without any holds barred whatsoever.

We should fight to win, and we should not go in for a limited war where we put our limited manpower against the unlimited hordes of Communist manpower which they are willing to expend lavishly, and do. They have no value for human life or respect for it at all.

If fight we must, let's go in there and shoot the works for victory with everything at our disposal.[3]

To "shoot the works for victory with everything at our disposal" may well blow us all up. It might produce a famous victory. But there might not be many left to applaud it, much less to realize the purpose for which it had been won. Soldiers, too, are servants, as are we all, of the deepest interests of our country, which demands among its highest charges upon us that we avoid and prevent atomic war. To do so force must always be controlled, limited, and directed to those ultimate interests.

3. THE BEARING OF DOMESTIC POLITICAL ISSUES AND PARTY
ATTITUDES UPON THE HAZARDS OF THE ATOMIC AGE.

One may agree in the main with the last section and yet say, "What has this got to do with party politics? Foreign

[3] *The Korean War and Related Matters.* Report of the Subcommittee to Investigate the Administration of the Internal Security Act and Other Internal Security Laws to the Committee on the Judiciary, January 21, 1955 (United States Government Printing Office, 1955), p. 7.

policy should be bipartisan or non-partisan. Politics should stop at the water's edge." Much has been done and much more can and should be done to bring about common understanding and agreement among us and our major parties on specific foreign policies and programs. Here the sound and right aim is to stand together and sink minor, and even some major, differences to gain the greater strength which comes from unity.

But unhappily it is not so simple as that. For often foreign policies cannot be separated from domestic policies. They are apt to be part and parcel of domestic issues upon which differences run very deep indeed.

Let us start with issues which arise out of differences in basic approach. Say that we are agreed that the purpose of foreign policy today is to create in the non-Communist world the power, unity, and will capable of balancing and checking the Sino-Soviet system, preserving our civilization, and preventing atomic war. The question then arises how we go at it. We all agree that we must "put first things first." But we do not agree what things are first things. In Henry Nevinson's preface to his delightful autobiography he writes: "I have always liked the Collect which prays that, among the sundry and manifold changes of the world, our hearts may surely there be fixed where true joys are to be found." And then adds: "To be sure, opinions differ innumerably as to what may be true joys, and how they should be approached."[4]

So it is with the question, which things are first? One view gives primary place to using our material, financial, and human resources to the extent necessary to give us the best chance of success in our basic purpose. The facts being what they are, this will produce a high level of expenditures and taxes. It means sacrifice at home for our policy abroad. The holders of this view believe that the country can afford whatever is necessary to preserve it.

Another view puts first in importance the balancing of the budget at a much lower figure, arrived at by giving weight to particular domestic considerations. This involves doing the best we can toward our basic purpose in the foreign field with the funds available within the lower budget figure. Its supporters dwell on the unhappy effects of high taxes and add that they speak with some authority because they pay a large part of them.

Some of the hardest-fought issues of party politics arise from these two approaches. The most enthusiastic advocates of bipartisan foreign policy would hardly conceive that bipartisanship could extend to the domestic issues involved. And yet from them flow the gravest consequences for foreign policy. The words remain the same

[4] Henry W. Nevinson, *Changes and Chances* (Harcourt, Brace and Company, New York, 1923), "Preface," p. v.

but the execution, which is what counts, will be very different depending on the level of material support, support not only for foreign programs as such but for our military and continental defense programs as well.

When we were discussing earlier the party attitudes toward the great depression, I pointed out that Mr. Hoover's Administration had believed that the federal government was limited in dealing with the problems which faced the country. It believed that it would be wrong for it to throw its own credit and resources into the gap left by the collapse of private, state, and municipal credit. I said also that Mr. Roosevelt's Administration accepted no such self-imposed limitation, that he conceived of the federal government as the whole people organized to do what had to be done. This also was the attitude of Mr. Truman's Administration when the Soviet atomic explosion in 1949 and the attack on South Korea in 1950 called for a drastic revision of foreign and military policy. Mr. Truman believed as strongly as anyone in reducing and balancing the budget. He had been remarkably successful in doing both. But fiscal considerations were not given by him the place of first importance. He was prepared to give them second place if that was necessary in doing what had to be done in the interest of national safety.

The present Administration appears to be acting upon the belief that fiscal considerations must be the governing ones. I will let Mr. Walter Lippmann describe what its attitude seems to be. Writing in January, 1955, of the President's budget and budget message, he says:

The controlling assumption is that we are at peace and that we may now make our plans on the expectation that peace will continue. The budget recognizes, of course, that the peace is insecure, that it rests upon an infirm balance of power and that, therefore, a very large expenditure (by peace time standards) for the armed forces is necessary. But the underlying assumption is, none the less, that the principles of a peacetime economy may now be applied. In no important sense do these principles need to be modified because of the cold war. The authors of the budget message do not in fact believe that there is any great practical difference between being at peace and being in a cold war.

. . . .

The budget message, with its overriding emphasis on balancing the budget at a lower level of taxes, does much to raise the question of whether the determining principle of the military policy has been military security or fiscal theory.

Nor would it be a serious exaggeration to say that in this budget, the exigencies of the cold war receive hardly more than token recognition. In the great competitive struggle as to whether the underdeveloped nations shall follow the one path or the other, the budget leaves Mr. Dulles and Mr. Stassen mighty little, except mimeographed statements, to compete with.[5]

[5] Walter Lippmann, "The Administration Mind," in the Washington *Post and Times-Herald,* January 20, 1955.

For my part, I believe that a view which gives fiscal and tax considerations this paramountcy is dangerous. Paramountcy should lie in the development of power relationships in the years in which we are now living. Sir Oliver Franks, recently British Ambassador to the United States, tells us in the first of his Reith Lectures:

I believe that history has given us a period within which to work out our problems. The period began with the end of the second world war and may last as long as the working lifetime of my generation. It will not be longer: it may well be shorter. Within the period no one year or the decisions made in it are likely to be in the strict sense crucial, neither this year, nor next year, nor the year after. Within the period there is always still time. But the whole period, whatever its duration may turn out to be, is crucial: what we do or fail to do in it will be decisive. After it there will be no second chance.[6]

In these crucial years the size of our budget and the considerations which determine its size and composition will be among the decisions which determine whether or not we work out our problems. Domestic issues, the subjects of party controversy, turn out to be at the very heart of our foreign policy and national security.

As I look at the parties, their past conduct, their composition and leadership, I believe that the Democratic

[6] Sir Oliver S. Franks, *Reith Lectures, Britain and the Tide of World Affairs* (Oxford University Press, New York, 1955), pp. 1-2.

party has the better prospect of grasping and acting on what I think are the fundamental truths and realities here. Clearly there will be political moves and counter-moves—there are, even as I write—which will confuse and obscure the issue. But this question of what should come first and what should come second is too pressing to remain obscured very long. What I think is the right answer will not come easily to a party based so exclusively upon business interests and the business point of view. It should not be strange to Democratic leaders or rank and file because it has been their party policy for almost their entire active lives. I see no reason for fainthearted-ness or doubt that they will continue to believe in it and carry a majority of their fellow citizens with them. Diffi-cultics there will be, for it is the harder course. But it is the course essential to winning through.

5

Foreign Policy Continued—

The Underlying Tasks

GRAVE as are the problems and dangers which nuclear physics has imposed upon international relations, there are plenty of others. Nuclear war is, as we suggested, the brooding omnipresence, under the shadow of which the nation-states impinge on one another. For they most certainly do impinge on one another. There is hardly an act of anyone—and words can be acts—which does not affect others and produce its responsive reaction. The whole group gives the impression of being bound together in a form of restless life in which forces are constantly pushing against other forces, constantly moving, changing, in search of balanced and maintained pressure. In spite of how they appear in the news, the relations of nation-states are not episodic and isolated; they are continuous and interrelated. And the criterion of importance is not what we say or write about what is done or not done, but how what is done or not done affects the results of these pushes and counter-pushes.

To get an idea of the nature and purpose of this inter-related life of states, consider, to begin with, the inter-national situation as it existed at the beginning of 1939. I am not suggesting that it was clearly discerned by any-one at that time, but, as the years went on, its outlines began to emerge.

A virtual monopoly of military power, or at least a vast superiority, was in the hands of three totalitarian states: Germany, Russia, and Japan. These states were contiguous and their purposes were hostile to the secu-rity of the Western democratic states. Together their mil-itary power could not be withstood, at least, if it should be exercised in Eurasia to accomplish purposes there. But, if Germany and Russia fell out, and the power of one of them was added to that of the Western states, the result might be very different, as indeed it was. That com-bination of power was sufficient, but only after the great-est exertion and sacrifice, to defeat Germany and Japan, with Italy thrown in.

But something else is much clearer now than it was then. It is that, if the power of Germany and Japan was destroyed, the power of Russia was bound to be greatly increased. This was likely to occur in part from the move-ment of Russian forces beyond the boundaries of the Soviet Union in the wake of defeated and retreating enemy forces. In part, also it would be made possible by postwar operations in areas of great weakness and fluidity created by the collapse of the defeated and occupied nations as well as the exhaustion of many of the victors:

If I may quote myself:

In other words, not only was the balance of power upset in 1939 but even a successful outcome of war would quite certainly leave it upset. And clearly it would remain upset unless the power of the United States continued vigorous and active. But United States military might could not alone prevent an erosion of power on one side and accretion on the other by subversion—working in exhausted societies and aided, when necessary, by the local use of force or threat of force.

So it became increasingly plain . . . that the United States was, and must remain, in and of the world, and that co-existence of the victors and the maintenance of peace demanded the recreation of a balancing power to the power of the Soviet system. It demanded a group of nations bound together by the most vital of common interests—their survival as free, independent nations—willing and able to join in maintaining the integrity and independence of the group; it demanded further that they be ready to help, encourage and if necessary protect other nations, even those not intimately associated with them, which had the one essential determination—to maintain their own independence.[1]

[1] Dean Acheson, " 'Instant Retaliation': The Debate Continued," *New York Times Magazine*, March 28, 1954, p. 13.

All of this, as I have said many times, became clear later on. It was not obvious during the tumult and exertions of war. A year after hostilities had ceased we could agree that a mot of Sir Willmott Lewis was applicable here. "We have chaos," he said, "but not enough to make a world." Perhaps there was enough, and what was lacking was omnipotence. The destruction of the military power of Germany and Japan removed the counterweights which had for many years balanced Russia and restrained its expansiveness. The power which had accomplished this destruction underwent division and disintegration. The Soviet Union, following Stalin's speech of February, 1946, adopted a policy independent of and hostile to the interests of its former allies. We and our Western allies demobilized our military forces. Perhaps it is more accurate to say that the people demobilized themselves. As a result the task of creating a balancing power system had to begin at the very bottom. In fact, so great had been the disruption of the war that, before one could create an alliance, it was necessary to create allies.

Upon these tasks United States foreign policy has been engaged since the end of the war. It is still engaged on them. They must remain a major purpose for years to come; for this purpose fits into and supplements that other major purpose discussed in the last chapter—the avoidance and prevention of nuclear war. In short, the

objective of our policy is to avoid and prevent a situation
in which we have to make a choice between surrender
and a nuclear war. For eight of the ten years since the
end of the war this work was carried on under Democratic leadership and responsibility. As we examine and
analyze what was done and what was necessary to get it
done, we shall, I believe, see some of the qualifications
of the party to do this work and, in the main, to do it
successfully.

The familiar list of actions and programs pretty well
shows the pattern of what was done and not done in the
recreation of a balancing power to the power of the
Soviet system. The British loan of 1946; the checking of
Soviet penetration of Iran, 1945-1946; the support of
Turkey against Soviet attempts to gain a foothold in the
Straits, 1946; the assumption of the burdens which the
British could no longer carry in helping Greece and Turkey maintain their independence, 1947; the joint action
with the nations of Europe through the Marshall Plan
to restore them to health and vitality, 1947-1951; the
assurance in two hemispheres that an attack against one
is an attack against all, 1947-1949; the defeat of the
blockade of Berlin, 1948-1949; the restoration of economic life and the return to the company of free nations
of Germany and Japan, 1949-1951; the steps to make
NATO an effective instrument of military defense, 1949-
1952; the effort by the Point Four program to bring help

to the underdeveloped areas and the new nations in their struggle for improvement for their people and stability for their national life, 1949-1952; the expansion of our own military strength and defense and that of our allies, 1950-1952; the military opposition to aggression in Korea through the United Nations, 1950-1952.

All this added weight to our side of the scales. So did the rebellion of Marshal Tito against the imperialism and subversion of Moscow. On the other side was added the great potential power of China when the collapse of the Nationalist regime and the flight of Chiang Kai-shek left the country by default to the Communists. I leave to others more detached than I the appraisal of the causes and contributory causes of this misfortune.[2] My own views, for what value they may possess, have been expressed elsewhere.[3]

The sweep, coherence, and energy of all that was done is hard to grasp from a mere catalogue of measures, or even to convey at all. The financial effort was immense. So were the production and military efforts. But these do not go to the heart of the real achievement. It lies, I

[2] High among them is Mr. Herbert Feis in his book, *The China Tangle* (Princeton University Press, 1953).

[3] Hearings before the Committee on Armed Services and the Committee on Foreign Relations, United States Senate, 82d Cong., 1st Sess., to Conduct an Inquiry into the Military Situation in the Far East and the Facts Surrounding the Relief of General of the Army Douglas MacArthur from His Assignments in That Area, Part 3, June 4, 1951, pp. 1837 *et seq.* (Government Printing Office, 1951).

think, in the boldness, the imaginativeness, the creative-
ness of the thinking, and perhaps most of all in
the will which those in charge maintained and com-
municated to the country. This stemmed straight from
President Truman himself. The sustained leadership and
effort put forth by the government and people of the
United States in these years represented a revolution in
American foreign policy and the assumption of burdens
and responsibilities wholly new to us.

Now all of us know, though too few seem to comprehend when it comes to foreign affairs, that wishing for
something does not achieve it. Ends which we want to
achieve are unlimited and not too hard to specify. But
the means by which to achieve them are not so easy to
come by. From earliest childhood we have all been told,
and learned all too painfully in our private affairs, that
"if wishes were horses beggars would ride."

So to define a goal is not to arrive at it. To do that requires the necessary means. The means necessary to
success in the great series of undertakings I listed had
to come from two sources. There were the means which
the United States could provide; and there were the
means which only the nations associated with us could
provide. Each was indispensable to success.

To provide the means within our own control and
power is a function of our own will. Much is possible if
our government and people will it. Little is possible if

we will it feebly or if we want something else more, such as to be released from the obligations of military service or to have taxes reduced and the budget balanced at a level inconsistent with the needed effort.

I do not mean to suggest that there is no limit to what we can accomplish as a nation by willing to do it. Blessed as we are in our heritage of human and material resources, they are not endless. We must be thrifty and sensible in our decisions. But, as a practical matter, we are confronted by a power combination which also has its limitations of resources, different from ours to be sure, but in total more severe; and it cannot be said that we are unable, if we will it, to do our part in creating and maintaining a counterbalancing power system.

This, of course, is reminiscent of what has been said in the last chapter, where the same point was made. It is fair to say that during the years we are now discussing this country, under strong leadership which made clear the need for effort and sacrifice, had the will to do what was within its power.

When we come to the second essential, the means which can be provided only by the governments and peoples associated with us, the requirement is still one of will. But it is not our will. Here other wills and interests beyond our control come into play. We can do much to persuade, inspire, assist, but we cannot command. Here the final word will be given by others. It will be expressive of other wills, or the lack of other wills. In pursuing the common task of preserving and increasing the power and vigor and unity of the nations still free, our country can help by furnishing the missing components, but not the component of national purpose, nor the will to remain free and to develop in its own way, however different from ours that may be.

The existence of this national purpose on the part of nations associated with us—a purpose to do all they can for themselves and in the common effort—does not remove all problems. It makes success possible but does not guarantee it. Many difficulties remain, not the least of them the problem of leadership in a coalition of free nations. Such a group operates on the basis of consent. Satellite nations are held together by coercion. The task of leadership in a free coalition is the task of obtaining and maintaining consent to common policies and programs.

There is a tendency on the part of some to assume the fact of United States leadership of the free world. We did not seek it, they say, we would be relieved if it could pass from us, but it has been thrust upon us. In other words, it comes from what we are and not from what we do. This, I think, is likely to lead us into error. Leadership is accorded where trust has been first given. And trust is dependent on conduct. It is cautiously given and quickly taken back. I think it wiser to believe that, as we inspire trust, consent will be given to policies which we advocate or support. But what do we mean by trust? We mean that we inspire confidence that the interests we are safeguarding embrace the interests of the people who trust us.

It is inevitable that allies and friends, owing to their differences in position, power, and experience, will have different attitudes of mind, different immediate preoccupations, differences in their interests and fears. The task is to build strength out of unity through policies and acts in which all can join because their interests are better served with them than without them, because the effort required of them is within their capacities, and because the common plan offers the best chance of success in the solution of the major common problems. A former colleague has wisely observed: "The essence of leadership is the successful resolution of problems and the successful attainment of objectives which impress themselves as being important to those whom one is called upon to lead."

Take as an illustration of successful leadership in this sense the conduct of the British, French, and United States governments in response to the blockade of Berlin. The blockade developed out of the reform of the currency in Western Germany and Russian determination to keep this currency out of East Berlin and Eastern Germany. I doubt that at the beginning the Russians intended a major challenge to the Western powers. Nevertheless a challenge resulted. When it did, rash action might have landed us and our friends in war. So all of us had the strongest interest in cool judgment, consultation, and action which was adequate and restrained. A course which satisfied these requirements would produce trust. Such a course was followed.

The issues—both over the currency and over the illegality of the Soviet restraints on land and water communication with Berlin—were put into the United Nations and discussed there. In the meantime the airlift to Berlin was instituted by United States, British, and French agreement. Also by agreement, countermeasures to interrupt traffic between East and West Germany were undertaken. The United States inevitably had to carry the largest burden but it did so with the full understanding and support of its friends. All agreed that Western rights in Berlin must be maintained and the West Berliners supported; all were satisfied that their lives and interests were not being unnecessarily risked by provocative or rash action; and—not least important—the course followed was successful.

On the other hand, consider as an act of leadership the announcement by the Secretary of State in January, 1954, of the policy of instant retaliation. Without consultation or warning, our allies were informed publicly that a new military policy had been decided upon and was in effect.

> So long [the spokesman said] as our basic policy concepts were unclear, our military leaders could not be selective in building our military power. If an enemy could pick his time and place and method of warfare—and if our policy was to remain the traditional one of meeting aggression by direct and local opposition—then we needed to be ready to fight in the Arctic and in the Tropics; in Asia, the Near East, and in Europe; by sea, by land, and by air; with old weapons and with new weapons.[4]

It was pointed out that to be equipped in this all-around military manner cost a great deal—a fact stated in the preceding chapter. But it was not pointed out that this "traditional" policy of meeting aggression where it occurred had something to be said for it, particularly as a policy for a coalition, or several coalitions, including many nations. To expect defense where the attack occurred gave hope, confidence, and enhanced sense of protection to nations in danger of aggression. Then again, it gave all the nations, including our own, the comforting assurance that those in charge in Washington were not thinking of blasting away with nuclear weapons at some place of their own exclusive choosing

[4] Secretary of State John Foster Dulles, "The Evolution of Foreign Policy," address before the Council on Foreign Relations, New York, January 12, 1954, *Dept. of State Bulletin*, Vol. XXX, No. 761, January 25, 1954, pp. 107, 108.

if aggression took place anywhere. The contrary impression would make them believe that, whatever Washington might think of its own interests, it was not giving much consideration to theirs.

Then the announcement of the new policy went on:

But before military planning could be changed, the President and his advisers, as represented by the National Security Council, had to take some basic policy decisions. This has been done. The basic decision was to depend primarily upon a great capacity to retaliate, instantly, by means and at places of our choosing. Now the Department of Defense and the Joint Chiefs of Staff can shape our military establishment to fit what is *our* policy, instead of having to try to be ready to meet the enemy's many choices. . . .[5]

This was something of a stunner to our friends. Apparently some pretty basic policy decisions had been made, and made unilaterally in Washington. "This," the speaker said, "has been done." It seemed that these decisions scrapped the "traditional" policy of defense where the attack occurred. Apparently, also, the decisions had favored "new weapons" over "old" ones. We were going to depend "primarily" upon a great capacity to retaliate and to do it "instantly," with no time wasted at all. Finally, this retaliation was to occur "by means and at places of our choosing." The word "our" was used twice in this paragraph and italicized the second time.

[5] *Ibid.*, p. 108.

Mr. Pearson, the Minister of External Affairs of Canada, was quick to ask what was meant by "our" choosing. Whose choosing was "ours"? It seemed that the word "instantly" answered the question. All in all the announcement produced in our friends and our allies agitation, doubts, fears, and loss of confidence in our leadership. In a short time it was diluted by a series of interpretations from Washington, mostly contradictory or qualifying. Confusion grew.

This is almost a classic illustration of the way a leader among free nations should not proceed. For it disregarded the most elementary precepts. First it threatened, or appeared to threaten, nuclear warfare. If, as we have seen, one of the basic goals of our policy is to avoid and prevent nuclear warfare, no subsidiary policy can be based on threatening to engage in it. If we mean to carry out the threat, we are false to a basic purpose; if we do not, we may cause dangerous miscalculation elsewhere. Another precept disregarded is not to proclaim policies which do not comprehend the interests of our friends, especially when they have not been consulted. These interests, so they believed, were not served by a policy which seemed to suggest that our primary dependence in meeting any aggression was instantly to precipitate something which seemed very like general war. A third is that policies formulated must be calculated to bring success in objectives which impress themselves as being important to our associates. The failure of this one was soon to be demonstrated.

"Let us now see," the speaker said, "how this concept has been applied to foreign policy, taking first the Far East. . . .

"I have said in relation to Indochina that, if there were open Red Chinese army aggression there, that would have 'grave consequences which might not be confined to Indochina.' "[6]

It is a fair inference from this statement that the new policy was applicable to Indochina and that favorable results were contemplated from its application. Unhappily Dienbienphu fell in four months' time and nothing was heard of the new policy. In addition to its other faults, it was a failure.

What has been said so far in our present chapter amounts to this: one of the chief purposes of American foreign policy, which supplements and is necessary to that other high purpose of avoiding nuclear war, is to develop the unity and strength of coalitions of free nations as a balance to the power of the Sino-Soviet system. At present this is our best reliance for living through troubled times without war while maintaining our own and our associates' vital interests. To play our part in these coalitions requires strong domestic leadership to sustain the will to do our own part, which is well within

[6] *Ibid.,* p. 108.

our national power. It requires also the capacity to understand the interests of our friends and to support and propose policies which make plain that their interests are truly served by association with us.

I believe that the Democratic party in our lifetime has shown the superior capacity to produce and support this leadership and that the Republican party is handicapped by its experience in this century and the tradition and division to which this experience has given rise. My hope is that the Democratic party in opposition and in power will continue to provide leadership which in the future, as in the past, holds firmly to the accomplishment of the central purposes without which all may be lost.

In doing this the party has the great asset mentioned in Chapter Two—its hospitality to intelligence. This is again illustrated by the conduct of our foreign relations in the years following the war. Ideas were welcomed and respected. Men capable of having them were welcomed, respected, and both stimulated and supported. In Washington and in the field a group, without regard to party affiliation, from inside and outside the permanent service, brought together uncommon ability, experience, and alertness.

The result was a renaissance of thought and inventiveness which was unexcelled—and it is not too much to say, unequaled—in any chancellery in the world. This was not the work of any one man, or of the several men who directed it from time to time. It was the work of the whole group supported by permanent services inspired and permitted to do the best that was in them. The policies and programs, developed and put into effect from 1946 to 1952, show the scope, the depth, and the power of the inventive thought brought to bear.

The effect of this environment of generative energy went beyond the Executive branch. It is seen, for instance, in the figure of Senator Arthur Vandenberg, which looms large in the postwar years. He had ability of the highest order. He was a master of advocacy and maneuver. He had the full respect and admiration of the Senate and the added strength of having been a severe critic of "foreign entanglements." But he did not have a particularly original or creative mind. His instincts were toward caution—to hold back, to examine the difficulties of the course proposed, and to restrain the enthusiasts.

These were good qualities. They were ideal qualities for a leader of an opposition which had for a part of the time control of the Congress. For he was dealing with an Administration which overflowed with ideas. He did not have to be creative or original. He did not have to furnish motive power. He was free to do what he could do best—criticize, question, examine—until he became convinced of the necessity for a proposed program. He would then put his unmistakable mark on it, and finally give it the essential help of his incomparable advocacy and fervor, the shrewd guidance of his knowledge of the Congress. One may ask whether his deserved reputation would have been so great had his years of influence and power on the Foreign Relations Committee been spent during an administration of his own party.

The years since 1952 in American foreign policy are not notable for the quality of the ideas generated. Policy has coasted on the momentum of past initiative. New situations have arisen by reason of the very success of past policies. They should not have been unexpected. Even before the death of Stalin, new Soviet tactics and strategy were forecast at the Communist Party Congress to meet the growing strength and unity of the Atlantic Community. When the aggression in Korea was defeated, it was to be expected that pressure would be increased at a softer and more profitable spot. But it is one thing to speak of having "seized the initiative" and quite another to know what to do with it. The stream of ideas, of imaginative thinking, had dried up. The power of energetic action seemed to have been lost.

One reason why this is so lies in the recurrent attempt of Republican legislators to whittle down the Executive and to subordinate its will to the Congressional will in foreign as well as domestic matters. There is enough mischief that follows an attempt in domestic matters to reduce the Presidency from a concurrent, coequal and co-ordinate branch of the government, to one that is

subordinate to the Congress. But the mischief is com-
pounded many times over when this is done in the field
of foreign affairs. The reasons have a structural origin.[7]
When our friends and adversaries present themselves to
us in complicated groupings; when the tides of diplomacy
make sudden shifts; when American and foreign troops
are under unified command; when the United States acts
as the focal point for a complex federation of military,
diplomatic, and economic allies, how can Congress provide the leadership for a concert of allied powers? It is
not structurally organized to exert that leadership. Information necessarily comes to it episodically and pre-
digested. It is not in continuous contact with foreign
leaders. It is not in a position to assess on a day-to-day
basis the opportunities and dangers which spring up in
remote places, and then to relate them to a happening
ten thousand miles away. The Congress, in short, is not,
was not intended to be, and cannot be an Executive.
Nevertheless, under Republican party doctrine, it per-
sists in trying to be one, with results that hobble the
Executive impulse in the conduct of foreign affairs.
What further splits the energy of the Executive—what
contributes to a confusion of policy—what fosters dis-
sensions—what slackens the force of public opinion in
censuring misdeeds, is when the Constitutional Execu-

[7] The summary statement about the contemporary limitations on
Congressional management of foreign affairs is drawn from Sidney
Hyman's book, *op. cit.*, pp. 273-274.

tive, under Republican theory, permits, and even encourages, the Legislature to encroach on powers that are not its own.

Certainly the power of energetic action has been lost in foreign economic policy—and lost for a very interesting reason. Here one can see that, while in human biology acquired characteristics are not inherited, in the biology of political parties the opposite may be the case. Without pressing the generalization, it does seem to be true that the Republican belief in the efficacy of high tariff protection has been inherited from earlier days and continues like the appendix, a menace to health after its function has ceased to exist.

With the South for some years after the Civil War no longer a political factor, the Republican North and West surrounded the United States with tariff walls. These grew ever higher as one administration succeeded another. Their necessity and efficacy became an article of faith. Meanwhile our mass production industry became firmly established, efficient, and in nearly all lines competitive with foreign producers. The Underwood Tariff of 1913 reversed the upward tariff trend, but its lower duties were largely inoperative, as the First World War turned foreign production to military channels and military operations interrupted trade. That war also changed the American position from one of a debtor nation, needing a balance of exports, to one of a creditor nation, requiring the opposite. Nevertheless, after the Republicans came to power, the Fordney-McCumber Act in 1922 imposed duties at new peaks. The leaders of the business community and the business point of view were still in accord with traditional Republican doctrine. In 1929-1930 President Hoover would have liked a downward revision and hoped for a time to get one. But the tide in his own party was too strong for him and the revision was upward.

A little more than a decade later, after the depression had run its course and the Democrats were in control, fissures began to appear in the Republican position. The Hull Reciprocal Trade Agreements program, conducted with Mr. Hull's typical caution and reasonableness, began to have some business support. Particularly the businessmen interested in foreign trade and farm producers of exported products could see a connection between dollars earned by foreigners from our imports and dollars spent by foreigners for our exports.

During the Second World War and its immediate aftermath the business community again was not conscious of competition from imports. The problem was to find means of financing the vast surplus of exports from America which to other countries, and particularly European countries, was their only hope of regaining productivity and strength. So during this period of nearly twenty years the tariff was not an issue pressing on the consciousness of the business community. Nor was it one which greatly agitated the Republicans in Congress. Broadly speaking, they made no spirited attack on the Reciprocal Trade Agreements legislation or its renewal when the Democratic majorities were large. When they were small, or the majority was the other way, they attempted various amendments (peril points, escape clauses, etc.) to limit its scope. But Congressional leaders showed reluctance to attack the law head-on.

The fissures which we began to see in the 1940's were now crevasses. Indeed, the new Administration in 1953, faced with the facts of international economic life, saw the necessity of reversing the historic doctrine of protection. "Trade not aid" became the slogan, and the Randall Commission, on the membership and staff of which the highest echelons of business and finance were strongly represented, went to work on the methods of increasing imports and foreign investment.

But it was one thing for the high command of business and party to decide that it was time for a change. It was quite another to convince the rank and file of the party, the general run of businessmen, and, most of all, the politicians who are experts on the beliefs of their constituents and usually a little behind them in changing direction. All Mr. Randall's skill, persuasiveness, and compromises did not suffice to lure the Republican Congressional leadership into the corral. The Trade

Agreement Act's very lease on life was kept a tenancy from year to year. Action under the Act came to a virtual stop. Relief from this situation came only from a Democratic Congress.

The traditions of three-quarters of a century and more are deep and resistant. Here again the Republican party is divided within itself just as business is divided within itself. A few in the highest positions see the new situation and the need for new policies to meet it. But the many cling to the doctrines in which they have been reared, doctrines for which the supporting arguments of self-interest can be made so speciously simple with the aid of selected statistics. Here again the Democrats have the advantage of greater unity, but not complete unity. The growing industrialization of the South exacted a high price as the Reciprocal Trade Agreements Act was amended in the Senate. But the unity is great enough so that under strong leadership, which was possible in the House in 1955, and which can be exercised by a Democratic President, liberal trade policies can be maintained and extended.

Not that liberal trade policies can solve all economic problems or that increased trade is a panacea. It is not. Peoples must have something to trade with before the process can go very far. And this, in turn, brings up the problem of foreign investment to increase the productivity of other parts of the world. I see no clear solution

here. On the one hand, time presses. Peoples are demanding results—and spectacular results—from their
governments. Unrest boils in some places, simmers in
others. On the other hand, why should the American
investor pass by the opportunities offered on this rela-
tively stable continent and risk his funds in countries
where, in addition to the business risk, he meets political
instability, the possibility of international conflict, na-
tionalism rampant, carrying with it, as it so often does,
the dislike and distrust of the foreigner?

Here again, theory must yield to the exigencies of our
own interest. We have a deep interest in the stability
and independence of many young governments brought
into existence by the newly won independence of their
people. Often memory of the past makes them suspicious
and wary of foreign help and, so we think, blind to real
dangers before them. Of one thing they are acutely
aware, the need for economic improvement, increased
production, higher standards of life. Private advice and
investment can be of great help. But it cannot bring the
minimum assistance which, in our own interest, is required. So theory must yield again to the conception, already mentioned, of our government as the whole people
organized to do what has to be done. This was the conception behind the Point Four program and the foreign
aid programs. Our government carried on these programs, not because it was theoretically desirable for gov-

ernment to do so rather than private business or private philanthropy, but because they would not be carried on at all unless government did so—and it was, and still is, essential that this help be given. And it should be given, not grudgingly, or with conditions attached, or as charity, but as a part of a broad and sensible foreign policy to achieve essential results, not to evoke gratitude.

On the whole matter of foreign economic policy these generalizations are not unfair: First, that it makes a lot of difference in what direction policy is pointing and how energetically it is pressed. Second, that Democratic policy, on the whole, makes for the economic health and vigor of the free coalitions, while Republican policy, which is stronger even than its own Administration, is a policy of foot dragging.

The present chapter and the one preceding have pointed out the important points in foreign policy where, so it seems to me, the difference in party attitudes, deeply rooted in their composition and history, may determine success or disaster in dealing with the perils among which we live. Sir Oliver Franks thought that the time we had in which to work out our problems was "the working lifetime of my generation. It will not be longer; it may well be shorter. . . . After it there will be no second chance." How long is that? Fifteen years? A decade? Perhaps less time than it will take a child beginning school to finish high school? Whatever the time may be it is pitifully short; it is fleeting; it must not be wasted. Years of doing the wrong thing, of putting second things first, cannot be brought back.

What we do in the time given us is decisive. "After it there will be no second chance."

6

The State and the Individual

1. THE MORAL BASIS OF FREEDOM

In a free society the relationship between the state and the individual—between authority and order, on the one side, and individual freedom and liberty, on the other—is never settled and fixed. It is a kinetic relationship, the resultant of constant struggle back and forth. And the nature of the struggle is not always a simple one; for the individual has a stake both in order, supported by authority, and in freedom. Authority is not inherently an enemy of liberty; indeed it is necessary to it. If all restraints were purely self-imposed, individual freedom would suffer in the resulting anarchy. So, individual freedom often depends upon a struggle to maintain authority or to extend the rule of law into new fields which have developed without its restraints. But often, too, powerful groups attempt in their own interest to use the authority of the state to impose restraints on other groups which the latter think go too far, and in which the more disinterested remainder see danger to the liberties of all. Then, too, the bureaucracy, through which the organized state acts, has interests of its own in extending its authority. Authority is a hardy growth. It is only by constant watchfulness and constant battle that the kind of authority and order is maintained under which individual freedom can flourish.

In the Communist world the struggle has been resolved wholly in favor of authority. Resistance to it, at least open resistance, has ceased. Conformity rules.

What is the state of affairs in the non-Communist world, in what we call the free world, and in our own country? How strong, how vigorous is belief in the moral foundations of freedom? We have already seen that so far as the physical elements of power are concerned, the free world is well equipped to hold its own with the Communist system. It is the intensity of our belief in the values upon which we claim to base our lives, our law, and our institutions which may be the controlling factor in the equation of power. For these values are challenged. Values which spring from our conception of the central importance of the individual spirit are flatly and bluntly denied by the Communist system.

When we say that our scheme of things is based upon the dignity and worth of the individual, what do we mean? Not that each of us is important to himself and that we would organize life to glorify egocentricity. It is rather that the fundamental meaning of human life is found in the individual where that life resides. We can develop this idea in various ways.

We can speak of the purpose of life as the pilgrimage from birth to death through a battleground between good and evil. The individual makes the pilgrimage to choose what is good and reject what is evil, to transcend appetites and achieve the aspirations of the spirit. To do this the individual must be free. It is only freedom of choice which makes the choice of good significant.

Or one can put it another way. The purpose of life is the endless seeking of the individual mind and spirit— the seeking for knowledge, for understanding, for perception, for beauty—seeking for its own sake. For this is the nature of the human spirit, its means of life without which it perishes. And to seek means to be free.

However we state it, the moral basis of our common civilization is founded on belief in the dignity and worth of the individual and the necessity for his freedom. This is what gives sanction to the great guarantees of freedom in our law, guarantees designed to fence off an area around the individual into which rulers, priests, and neighbors may not enter to enforce conformity.

The Communists challenge this conception with contempt. The individual is worth nothing, a wretched, feeble creature whose mind and spirit can be bent and broken, trained by repetition and terror to accept any thought or to act in any way decided by those who can play upon the keyboard of his mind and appetites. "Even the greatest recalcitrants can, in fact, be conditioned to heap abuse upon themselves and confess to crimes that they never committed while praising their accusers."[1] To the Communists men are born to be used by those who have the strength and will to use them to accomplish the purposes of the Party, and through the Party, of the state.

But lack of belief in the dignity and worth of the individual is not confined to the Communists. There are vast populations where the conditions of life are so hard and depressed that all interest is centered on how to get enough food, warmth, and shelter to sustain life. It was to help lift this servitude and open the way to freedom that the Point Four program was proposed in President Truman's inaugural address. The essential thing about it was that it proposed

the use of material means to a non-material end. It is not that we believe that other people need or wish things for their own sake, merely to have these material objects. It is not that the material objects in and of themselves make a better or

[1] Louis J. Halle, *Civilization and Foreign Policy* (Harper & Brothers, New York, 1955), p. 167.

fuller life, but they are the means by which people can obtain freedom, not only freedom from the pressure of those other human beings who would restrict this freedom, but help in the ancient struggle of man to earn his living and get his bread from the soil. That is the purpose; that is the objective of this program.[2]

And in more advanced societies can we honestly say that belief in human dignity and worth is such a burning and moral conviction that it adds decisively to our physical strength?

. . . a "science" of mass communication and manipulation of the mass mind has been developing. Propagandists, public relations experts, sociologists, and advertisers have been learning how to condition (or train, or indoctrinate) "the public" so that it will support a certain policy and oppose another, so that it will demonstrate for one man and against another. . . . For some among us the badge of democracy is no longer diversity but uniformity.[3]

There is nothing new in the appeal to passion and prejudice by falsehood and fraud. Until our own time it has been done more by gifted amateurs than by professionals trained in a science, evil in its cynical basis that the individual upon whose dignity and worth we build our free society is merely an indistinguishable part of a mass to be manipulated. When there are added to the

[2] Dean Acheson, statement to the press, January 26, 1949.
[3] Halle, op. cit., pp. 167-168.

techniques of this new science the coercive powers of the state, then the drive for uniformity assumes imposing proportions. Unhappily this has been done, and, ironically enough, done in the name of making us more secure against the Communist challenge to our belief in the freedom of the individual. As the French proverb tells us: "Chacun prend à l'adversaire, qu'il le veuille ou non." (Everyone takes on the face of his adversary, whether he wills it or not.)

2. THE COMMUNIST CONSPIRACY

The adversary which alarms us and impresses its face upon us is the Communist power system. It is a powerful system of nation-states which, as we have seen, presents to us dangers and problems of a military and political nature. It poses still another in our domestic affairs, in this very field of the relation between the individual and the state. The problem arises from the fact that a powerful group of states has as an ally the ideology of Communism. This ideology wins converts in foreign countries, including our own. These converts tend to band together in conspiratorial groups under the discipline of Moscow or Peiping. They become, depending on their strength, and any weakness which may exist in the surrounding society, useful aids to the foreign policy of Communist states. Some of them have engaged in espionage, but more often through labor unions, which they penetrate, or political parties, and through press and propaganda, they attempt to divide opinion and disrupt action in industry and politics. Where they become strong, as in France and Italy, it is due to deep dissatisfactions within the country. There they are a danger to the stability and security of the state. On the other hand, in the United States and Great Britain they are weak because the necessary conditions for the growth of Communism do not exist. The Attorney General tells us that in this country the members of the Communist Party number 23,000. They have no hold on or appeal to the American people. Here they are not a danger to the stability of the state. They do present dangers to its security. These dangers can be dealt with by action wholly consistent with our great traditions of individual liberty and dignity. To impair the liberty we are seeking to protect, through fear of subversion by so small a group, would be as foolish as it would be tragic.

It is a new and disturbing experience for living Americans to find even a small group here willing to be used as tools by a foreign state. But it is not new in American history. It happened during the French Revolution. Then, too, we responded to the experience with exaggerated fear, and dealt with it by the Alien and Sedition Acts of the Adams Administration. That effort accomplished more by way of impairing the liberty of loyal citizens than in curbing foreign agitators and fellow travelers. It is not an episode upon which we look back with pride. Unfortunately we failed to remember the lessons which it taught.

The first of these is that people who allow themselves to be frightened into hysteria and general distrust make fools of themselves, lose the respect of others, and usually perpetrate grave injustice. We forgot this lesson after the First World War when the bombing of Attorney General Palmer's house led to widespread fear of "radicals" of all sorts, and an orgy of repressive measures against them culminating in the expulsion of the Socialist members of the New York Legislature. Few emerged from this period of fright with credit, but among those few stands as a figure of sanity, courage, and justice, Mr. Charles Evans Hughes. We forgot the lesson again in 1950. Our real cause for concern over the discovery of the spy ring in Canada, of espionage in our atomic plants, and of a series of attempts, some successful and some not, to penetrate other branches of the government was played upon then for political purposes and fanned into the campaign of distrust discussed in Chapter Four. It was and is against this background that the last Administration and the present one have had to deal with the problems posed by these Communists. Its warping effect has gravely affected the liberty of the individual in and out of government to think and speak as he pleases and to live and work in the creative atmosphere of freedom and respect.

The administration of the internal security laws and regulations has raised a series of problems—constitutional, legal, administrative, and, most importantly, political. There is a constant tendency to resolve them all into questions to which courts can give us the conclusive and satisfying answers. More than a century ago de Tocqueville told us of ourselves: "Scarcely any political question arises in the United States that is not resolved, sooner or later, into a judicial question."[4] I do not propose to do that here, to argue whether certain procedures conform to the requirements of due process of law and would or would not be sustained by the courts. Nor is it the purpose of this discussion to consider the changes in the laws and regulations which are urgently needed. These present many perplexing problems; but the problems can and will be solved if an underlying political environment of faith in the freedom and dignity of the individual is restored. Without that environment, legal changes are ineffective and frustrated.

The ultimate reliance for the deepest needs of civilization must be found outside their vindication in courts of law; apart from all else, judges, howsoever they may conscientiously seek to discipline themselves against it, unconsciously

[4] Alexis de Tocqueville, *Democracy in America* (Alfred A. Knopf, Phillips Bradley Ed., New York, 1945), Vol. I, p. 280.

are too apt to be moved by the deep undercurrents of public feeling. A persistent, positive translation of the liberating faith into the feelings and thoughts and actions of men and women is the real protection against attempts to straitjacket the human mind. Such temptations will have their way, if fear and hatred are not exorcised. The mark of a truly civilized man is confidence in the strength and security derived from the inquiring mind. We may be grateful for such honest comforts as it supports, but we must be unafraid of its incertitudes. Without open minds there can be no open society. And if society be not open the spirit of man is mutilated and becomes enslaved.[5]

An arena in which this "persistent, positive translation of the liberating faith into the feelings and thoughts and actions of men and women" must take place is the arena of our public life, of public debate and decision on the great issues of government and liberty, the arena of politics.

3. THE EVILS WE HAVE BROUGHT UPON OURSELVES

The tradition of the American citizen is a proud one. As Elmer Davis reminds us, he was born free. He was sovereign. He called no one master. He need stand abuse from no one. He was entitled to say, "L'état, c'est moi!" But today that is changed. His government approaches him not as his agent and creature, but aloof, hostile, sus-

[5] Mr. Justice Frankfurter, in *Dennis* v. *United States*, 341 U.S. 494, 556.

picious. He cannot undertake an office under the federal government until a police agency has investigated him and "cleared" him. In doing this it establishes a dossier on him, going into his community, interviewing his friends and enemies, his business associates and rivals, his present and past employers, the town gossips—every source—and writing it all down, good, bad, and indifferent—all as reflected through the mind of an FBI agent. If the appointing or confirming authority is timid, the dossier may cause worry that the candidate may be a "controversial figure,"[6] which is itself a disqualification. In that case the appointment is quickly dropped, leaving an aura of doubt surrounding the unhappy candidate, who can find out nothing.[7]

But he may rightly feel some apprehension, for the

[6] "It is vital that the people of the United States have confidence in their representatives to the United Nations Assembly. Issues of critical importance affecting Asia will soon be before that body. Dr. Jessup has not got the confidence of our people. He is a controversial figure. His confirmation, I fear, would divide the country at a time when above all else we need unity." Statement by Senator H. Alexander Smith, *New York Times*, October 19, 1951, p. 6.

"Still, the Senator [Gillette] added, there was a lack of public confidence in Dr. Jessup, even though this might be mainly due 'to the concerted campaign of unfair and unprincipled attacks made on him.' While the present situation might be 'very unjust' to the Ambassador, Mr. Gillette declared, it, nevertheless, existed and on that ground he should not go to the United Nations." *New York Times*, October 19, 1951, p. 6.

[7] This was not the case in regard to the appointment of Dr. Jessup to the United States Delegation to the sixth session of the United Nations General Assembly. President Truman insisted upon a recess appointment.

dossier has a most ambivalent nature. Sometimes it is insisted that it is a mere collection of statements and reports which are not "evaluated" and must remain wholly secret. On other occasions, however, portions of the dossier are made public in one form or another—and often by persons who are not supposed to have access to it. On still other occasions it is said publicly, and with much head-shaking, that a large file exists on this person or that, and this fact alone is suggested as a disqualifying factor.

The use of a secret police dossier by the state against its citizens is capable of infinite variations and subtleties. It is and always has been a source of great power. Until we imposed this system on ourselves, it was used here only for criminals. And we imposed it on ourselves because our concern about a small conspiratorial group of Communists was fanned, as I have said, into distrust of one another—an intolerable attitude for a free people.

Not only are we subject to investigation, time and again, by a secret police but all of us may be investigated by our own representatives in the Congress whenever it suits their fancy. And they, too, through the Committee on Un-American Activities of the House of Representatives maintain a dossier system of their own. The more ill-mannered and boorish members of investigating committees may bully and browbeat us without arousing visible indignation or resentment. Even a respected officer of the Army, charged with no offense, may be told that he is not fit to wear the uniform.

The secret investigation is a first step from which other proceedings may follow. Charges may be made by the government resulting in the destruction of a citizen's good name and all that goes with it by labeling him as of doubtful loyalty or a risk to the security of the nation, on the basis of evidence of which he is not told, received from persons whom he is not allowed to confront, and of which only an anonymous summary is given to his judges.

Against procedures such as these the Kentucky Resolutions of November, 1798, thundered:

... that if the acts before specified should stand, these conclusions would flow from them; that the general government may place any act they think proper on the list of crimes and punish it themselves whether enumerated or not enumerated by the constitution as cognizable by them: that they may transfer its cognizance to the President, or any other person, who may himself be the accuser, counsel, judge, and jury, whose *suspicions* may be the evidence, his *order* the sentence, his *officer* the executioner, and his breast the sole record of the transaction. . . .[8]

These practices had their root in the President's Executive Order, 9835, of March 21, 1947. This order and the

[8] *The Writings of Thomas Jefferson* (G. P. Putnam's Sons, New York, Ford Ed., 1892-99), Vol. VII, pp. 289, 302.

Act of August 26, 1950, upon which rests the present Executive Order, 10450, of April 27, 1953, were adopted under a Democratic Administration. I was an officer of that Administration and share with it the responsibility for what I am now convinced was a grave mistake and a failure to foresee consequences which were inevitable. That responsibility cannot be escaped or obscured. It is true that these measures had strong bipartisan and popular support, indeed insistence, behind them. It is true, also, that the present Republican Administration, and particularly Attorney General Brownell, has continued, defended, and expanded the most harmful aspects of the loyalty program long after their destructive and corrosive consequences were plainly apparent. This does not absolve the Democratic Administration, but it should crowd the mourners' bench.

There is no more vigorous and determined defender of the faith than President Truman. He stated and acted on that faith in his veto message of September 22, 1950, on the Internal Security Act of 1950:

And what kind of effect would these provisions have on the normal expression of political views? Obviously, if this law were on the statute books, the part of prudence would be to avoid saying anything that might be construed by someone as not deviating sufficiently from the current Communist-propaganda line. And since no one could be sure in advance what views were safe to express, the inevitable tendency would be to express no views on controversial subjects.

The result could only be to reduce the vigor and strength of our political life—an outcome that the Communists would happily welcome, but that freemen should abhor.

We need not fear the expression of ideas—we do need to fear their suppression.

Our position in the vanguard of freedom rests largely on our demonstration that the free expression of opinion, coupled with government by popular consent, leads to national strength and human advancement. Let us not, in cowering and foolish fear, throw away the ideals which are the fundamental basis of our free society.[9]

The President believed that his Executive Order could and would be carried out with fairness and restraint, that, as he said, "loyal government employees should be protected against accusations which were false, malicious or ill-founded."[10] But his expectations were not fulfilled by the multitudinous administrators of the loyalty program, pressed, as they were, by the emotions generated by the reckless political attack on the Administration. Furthermore, it was not realized at first how dangerous was the

[9] Message from the President of the United States Returning Without Approval the Bill (H.R. 9490) to Protect the United States Against Certain Un-American and Subversive Activities by Requiring Registration of Communist Organizations, and for Other Purposes, Sept. 22, 1950, 81st Cong., 2d Sess., House Doc. No. 708, pp. 6-7.

[10] President Harry S. Truman, address before the Federal Bar Association, Washington, April 24, 1950, *Department of State Bulletin,* Vol. XXII, No. 566, May 8, 1950, pp. 707, 708.

practice of secret evidence and secret informers, how alien to all our conceptions of justice and the rights of the citizen, even though he was also an employee. Experience proved again how soon good men become callous in the use of bad practices. Familiarity breeds more than contempt, it breeds indifference. What was, at first, designed for cases which it was thought would be serious, sensitive, and rare, became commonplace and routine. Now in cases involving no secret agent or sensitive position, a person may be branded as of doubtful loyalty and dismissed on evidence by persons whose identity not even his judges know and whose words, summarized for them, are withheld from the defendant. Nor is this practice restricted to cases involving the employer-employee relation between the government and the defendant. It can apply also to private employment and to a citizen seeking a passport which the government requires before he may travel abroad.

In the seventeenth and eighteenth centuries our forefathers learned from bitter experience that this use of secret evidence by the state against the individual led to tyranny, destroyed the liberty of the citizen and was not to be endured. We are in the process of relearning that lesson. We shall learn, too, as they did, that every day, week, and month that wrong practices are continued makes them more difficult to correct. They become ingrained, not only in bureaucratic procedures, but in the thinking of our people, in and out of government. These practices spread like a cancer into parts of the system previously healthy.

Take, for instance, the determination of whether a Foreign Service officer's professional conduct has or has not conformed to the required standards of his profession. For years the law has provided that charges of this sort—both charges of incompetence or neglect and of wrongful action—shall be heard before the Foreign Service Board, whose members have full knowledge of the standards required of these officers. But recently this procedure has not been followed in cases of officers who have been publicly attacked because of their part in events which have since become politically controversial. Instead they have been charged by the Department which employed them, supervised them, and promoted them, with being either disloyal or security risks or both.

In the recent case of John Paton Davies a Special Security Hearing Board, with the Secretary of State concurring, found as to this officer of the highest standing and reputation that his "lack of judgment, discretion, and reliability raises a reasonable doubt that his continued employment in the Foreign Service of the United States is clearly consistent with the interests of national security."[11] Accordingly, he was dismissed.

[11] Statement by Secretary Dulles, November 5, 1954, *Department of State Bulletin*, Vol. XXXI, No. 803, November 15, 1954, pp. 752, 753.

One would assume, of course, that the "lack of judgment, discretion, and reliability" must be serious indeed to involve the national security. But the Secretary of State declared merely that in the Board's opinion the officer's "observation and evaluation of the facts, his policy recommendations, his attitude with respect to existing policy, and his disregard of proper forbearance and caution in making known his dissents outside privileged boundaries were not in accordance with the standard required of Foreign Service officers and show a definite lack of judgment, discretion and reliability."[12]

Now the board which made these critical findings about a Foreign Service officer's professional work was composed of persons who had no professional knowledge of the standard required of Foreign Service officers or of the foreign policy problems under which they condemned the officer's judgment, discretion, and reliability. The persons composing it were the Inspector General of the Army, the administrative officer of the Office of Defense Mobilization, a lawyer in the Federal Communications Commission, the Executive Secretary of the Public Advisory Committee of the Foreign Operations Administration, and the Director of the Office of Procurement and Technical Assistance of the Small Business Administration. These men, excellent as they undoubtedly were in their own fields, were given the task

[12] *Ibid.*, p. 753.

of judging the professional competence of a Foreign Service officer whom his professional colleagues and superiors had rated among the small group at the top.

The officer's only specified delinquency, so far as we are told, was "making known his dissents outside privileged boundaries." However reprehensible and subject to disciplinary action this may have been, it can hardly be said to imperil the security of the nation. For Mr. James Reston pointed out in the *New York Times*[13] that the Secretary who imposed the penalty "is personally the greatest dissenter outside of privileged boundaries in the recent history of the United States Capital. He has gone to more dinners with the reporters and registered more dissents from established policy in the last ten years than any official in this town."

And if errors of judgment are to be equated with security risk, very few of us could be regarded as secure, including Presidents, Generals, and Secretaries of State. To do so is again to "take on the face" of our adversary. The trial of Foreign Service officers for disloyalty or security risk, or both, because their views ten years ago are now regarded as heretical by a politically powerful and obstreperous group, is a purge no different from the Moscow type, except that the Foreign Service officers offer no threat to the regime in control. If error is insecurity, Mr. Reston asks, who determines what is error and by what

[13] November 10, 1954.

standard? For instance, he says, the same Secretary who found the Foreign Service officer's judgment to be in error would himself be regarded by a large body of professional diplomatic opinion as guilty of defective "judgment and discretion in handling the nation's enemies and allies before the partition of French Indochina," or "when he made his now famous threat of 'massive retaliation' against the Communist world" or "when he threatened the French with an 'agonizing reappraisal' before the French Chamber voted on the European Defense Community."[14] This does not, of course, impugn the Secretary's security status, though it may be said to cast doubt on his ability to draw a discerning line between good judgment and bad.

Now the plain fact is that, when this case was reduced to its real issues, the national security was not involved at all. The Board's findings and the Secretary's concurrence deal only with the professional propriety and quality of the officer's reporting, recommendations, attitude toward existing policy and relations with the press. In judgments of this character there is no place for police methods, non-professional judgment, and overtones involving national security. To bring them in is another sign of the obsession with subversion which has come over us. The long-existing provisions of the Foreign Service Act are wholly adequate for problems of this sort—

[14] *Ibid.*

and, incidentally, designed to produce just and wise dispositions of the cases, protecting both the government service and the officer.

Moreover, obsessive fear of subversion in our midst has gone further than to introduce the psychology of the purge into public employment. It has brought under suspicion and doubt what has been since the founding of this Republic the fundamental article of the American faith and the bulwark of individual liberty, the Bill of Rights set out in the first ten Amendments to the Constitution. In an address at Washington University the Chief Justice of the United States, Mr. Warren, referred to an episode which should give pause to us all:

A few days ago I read in the newspaper that a group of state employees . . . charged with responsibility for determining what announcements could be posted on the employees' bulletin board refused to permit the Bill of Rights to be posted on the ground that it was a controversial document. It was reported that the altercation became intense, and that only after the Governor in writing vouched for its non-controversial character was the Bill of Rights permitted to occupy a place along with routine items of interest to the state employees. And this happened in the United States of America on the 15th day of December, 1954, the 163rd anniversary of our Bill of Rights, declared by proclamation of President Eisenhower to be Bill of Rights Day.

It is straws in the wind like this which cause some thoughtful people to ask the question whether ratification of the Bill of Rights could be obtained today if we were faced squarely with the issue.[15]

Former Senator Harry P. Cain, now a member of the Subversive Activities Control Board set up under the Internal Security Act, notes the same trend. In a recent address, well worth careful study, he says:

Those who use "Fifth Amendment" as an adjective of disapprobation modifying the noun "Communist" are as guilty of disrespect for the Constitution as any Communist could be.

Centuries of inquisitional tortures, mental and physical, and misgivings over man's inhumanity to man forged and tempered the bulwark of freedom that the individual shall not be required to convict himself. We should be less concerned by the few who hide behind the privilege without justification and much more concerned by those who trifle with and prostitute its significance.[16]

Finally, in our summation of what is wrong, there is one comprehensive evil, the sum of all the others. It is the compulsion toward conformity. Literally thousands of minor officials in millions of cases apply rules of thumb provided by handbooks, to determine compliance

[15] The Honorable Earl Warren, "The Blessings of Liberty," address at Washington University, St. Louis, February 19, 1955.
[16] The Honorable Harry P. Cain, "Strong in Their Pride and Free," address before the Seventh Annual Conference on Civil Liberties, Washington, D. C., March 18, 1955, p. 7.

with scores of security and loyalty standards. They apply to public and much private employment from the lowliest to the highest positions, to travel from and into the country. They are capable of extension through the specious logic of fear and its exploitation to almost any activity of our daily life. One must not suppose that the run-of-the-mine officials who do this work are ill-disposed to our great traditions of individual liberty. They are merely taking care of themselves and their own jobs. In doing so, they must look askance at diversity, originality, heterodoxy of all sorts. They, too, are victims of the compulsion to conform.

4. WHAT IS THE ACTUAL DANGER AND FROM WHOM?

We have looked briefly at some, but by no means all, of the evils which our internal security system has produced. Let us now look at the actual danger which has led us into a course so destructive of our traditions and institutions.

It is, of course, the danger of espionage and sabotage. This comes either from professionals who are employed by a foreign state or those who serve a foreign state because they have put themselves for ideological reasons under its control and discipline. The danger may be from those actually engaged in this work or from those who are potential recruits.

So far as actual spies and saboteurs are concerned, are

the internal security procedures necessary or important in discovering and dealing with them? The answer clearly is that they are not. Three years after the first procedures were established in 1947, Mr. Seth Richardson (Assistant Attorney General in the Hoover Administration), Chairman of the Loyalty Review Board, reported to Congress, "Not one single case, or evidence directing towards a case, of espionage has been disclosed in that record."[17] If these procedures have uncovered any since, I have not heard of them. Spies and saboteurs are uncovered and apprehended by detective work called counter-espionage. To convict and punish them requires a trial court in which the accused is confronted by all the witnesses against him. Secret evidence is no help here. Moreover, I doubt whether any informed person would seek to justify the employee security programs as a means of catching spies and saboteurs. It is supported, rather, as a means of protection against persons, employed or candidates for employment, who might become spies or be used by spies. It is the potential rather than the actual and active against which these programs are in fact designed.

Now this opens up a pretty broad field. At least it does if we look at the sorts of people whom the regulations list as presenting dangerous possibilities. The spectrum disclosed is a long one. At the darker end are

[17] State Department Employee Loyalty Investigation Hearings, Subcommittee of the Committee on Foreign Relations, Senate, 81st Cong., 2d Sess. (1950) Part 1, p. 409.

members of the Communist party and those who are under the discipline of the Communist party whether or not it can be proved that they are formal card-carrying members. In the middle of the spectrum are those to whom the regulations attribute sympathy with Communist doctrines and programs by reason of their associations or their words written or oral. At the lighter end of the spectrum are persons who are thought to have weaknesses of character or situation upon which agents of a foreign power might prey.

Experience has shown, I believe, that these categories are in part wrong in composition, in part too vague to administer with justice, and, by the very numerical magnitude of those they are thought to embrace, defeat the purpose of the regulations by distracting attention and effort from substantial to negligible dangers.

Consider, to begin with, those at the lighter end of the spectrum who are usually called security risks rather than loyalty cases—the ones who have personal weaknesses or weaknesses in their situations. They cause concern not because they are suspected of any sympathy with Communism but because it is feared that they are peculiarly subject to pressure from blackmail or otherwise and may betray secrets. This belief seems to rest rather on *a priori* reasoning than statistical support.

. . . That the homosexual is peculiarly prone to commit crimes under the threat of blackmail is hardly doubted by

anyone who faces the problem for the first time. Yet neither
the histories of diplomacy and of treason nor the recollections
of practitioners of diplomacy, insofar as I could ascertain, contain an instance of a homosexual having committed an act of
treason under the threat of blackmail.

That an official who has relatives living behind the Iron
Curtain is particularly susceptible to committing treason
under blackmail sounds on the face of it so plausible that it
is virtually accepted as self-evident. But who knows of an
official who has violated security regulations under such circumstances? Here again, what on the face of it looks like
common sense reveals itself on closer examination as super-
stition which unchallenged repetition has vested with the
plausibility of truth.[18]

But, whether or not the concern about these people is
well founded, there is no necessity for their being caught
up in the dragnet of "security cases," with the connota-
tions of conduct bordering on disloyalty and incipient
treason. The essence of the complaint against them is
not that they are offenders who, to protect the national
security, must be branded with a badge of shame. It is
that they are unsuitable for the tasks they are performing
or may be called upon to perform. One who has a rela-
tive in Russia, or who talks too much, or drinks too much

[18] Hans J. Morgenthau, "The Impact of the Loyalty-Security Measures on the State Department," *Bulletin of the Atomic Scientists*, Vol.
XI, No. 4, April, 1955, pp. 134, 136.

is not a person to be punished or impeded in finding suitable employment. He is punished and impeded if his case is considered and determined in terms of the national security instead of what it really is, a case of suitability for his employment.

Cases of this sort can and should be dealt with in a sensible, just, and humane way. It is wholly unnecessary and inexcusable to treat the employees involved as incipient criminals. There is no need for "charges" filed against the employee, suspension from work (which in a great number of cases requires resignation under a cloud in order to live), appointment of a trial board, evidence, briefs, and decisions couched in terms of security. Fair and experienced employee administration can get at the facts, which are not often in wide dispute, and work out just disposition—reassignment to suitable tasks, or, if necessary, resignation or dismissal in accordance with usual Civil Service procedures.

But this can only be done amidst a public which remains cool, recognizes that the danger from the sort of people we are now discussing is slight and demands administration which respects the dignity and worth of the individual. If the atmosphere is a hysterical one, one in which political capital is made out of fear of Communists at home, one which sees in every human weakness an opening for Communist penetration, then the administrator becomes timid. He trembles lest it be said of him that he is soft on security risks. His chief interest is to pass on the responsibility for a case to someone else, with a recommendation protecting himself from any future criticism.

The rest of the spectrum includes people who are thought in one way or another to have some connection with the Communist party or interest in Communism. They run all the way from members of the party to those who, as the Atomic Energy Commission describes them, have a "sympathetic interest in totalitarian, Fascist, Communist, or other subversive political ideologies" or a "close continuing association with individuals (friends, relatives or other associates) who have subversive interests and associations. . . ."[19]

Now members of the Communist party have been found guilty of crime under our laws because they were organizers or members of a group advocating the overthrow of our government by force or violence with knowledge of its purpose. (*Dennis* v. *United States*, 341 U.S. 494.) In the popular mind this is a crime akin to treason. The good name and reputation of anyone found by the government to be associated with this group is irretrievably damaged. The individual's ability to earn a livelihood may be destroyed. In other words, it is a very serious matter indeed to make charges involving the "loyalty"

[19] AEC Policy Statement on Security Clearance for Personnel, issued January 5, 1949, as quoted in the *Bulletin of the Atomic Scientists*, Vol. XI, No. 4, April, 1955, pp. 159, 160.

of a citizen, far more so than the indictment of the individual for many crimes. One would suppose that if ever the citizen should be entitled to the historic requisites of a fair hearing, the opportunity of knowing the evidence against him, and confronting the witnesses, it is here.

This becomes increasingly clear when we think further about the charges based on "sympathetic interest" in Communism or association with others said to have it. At this point we begin to see how much of the definition of the charge and determination of its proof must rest in the subjective mind of those making the charge and the decision, in a "judgment or intuition more subtle than any articulate major premise."[20] To many people a Communist, disloyal, subversive, or untrustworthy person, is anyone holding unfamiliar, unconventional (and, therefore, disturbing, often frightening) views on economic, political, or social questions, or nuclear weapons. So, although we all use the same words, the variety of meanings attached to these words cover a very wide scope indeed.

For instance, in two *causes célèbres* of recent years—those of Dr. Robert Oppenheimer and Mr. John Paton Davies—those who drafted the charges were thoroughly familiar with the so-called "derogatory information,"

[20] Oliver Wendell Holmes, Dissenting Opinion in *Lochner* v. *New York*, 198 U.S. 45, 76.

which means the adverse evidence. In both cases they charged that this amounted to disloyalty to the United States. Yet in both cases all who sat in judgment were explicit that there was no evidence of disloyalty.[21] Instead they found that the accused were guilty of poor judgment and defects of character. The alleged defects of character were hardly in the class of those charged by many candidates for elective office against their opponents, as, for instance, the accusations against the successful candidate for Governor of New York in 1954. It is as though one were charged with murder and found guilty of rudeness—all on the same evidence.

In short, there is no real agreement on what the charge means; on what such words of accusation as "disloyal," "not consistent with the national security," etc., mean. There is no objective standard by which to draw conclusions in terms of these words from the evidence in these cases which, so far as it is known, is largely circumstantial and largely hearsay. In this situation, only

[21] It may be said that Commissioner Thomas E. Murray should be excluded from this broad statement. Perhaps; but let us see. Mr. Murray declared in his concurring opinion, "the primary issue is the meaning of loyalty." For those in Oppenheimer's position, he said, "their faithfulness to the lawful government of the United States, that is to say their loyalty, must be judged by the standard of their obedience to security regulations." Oppenheimer was guilty, he found, of "a frequent and deliberate disregard of the security regulations which restrict a man's associations" and "seriously deficient in his cooperation with the workings of the security system." Therefore "he was disloyal."

In my view Mr. Murray is not an exception at all.

through adversary proceedings, in which the evidence is analyzed and the witnesses cross-examined, can judges, prosecutor, the accused, and the public know what is really at issue and the basis of fact or opinion on which the decision rests. The Oppenheimer and Davies cases show that it is better to open some of the evidence to this process than not to open any of it. But they show also that to keep some evidence secret casts an aura of mystery over the final decision. It never wholly stands upon its declared reasons. There is always the attitude on the part of the officials, "if you knew what I know but can't tell," lurking in the background. The taint of injustice infects the whole proceeding.

As we examine this portion of the spectrum of loyalty cases, the basic fallacy in the program begins to emerge. In our concern over the danger from the Communist conspiracy, we have been driven to a search for an illusion, the illusion of complete security. We have attempted to list and guard against every external symptom of behavior of a mind which, under any conceivable circumstances, might be led, beguiled, deceived, or blackmailed into wittingly or unwittingly betraying secrets of the government. This is and always was an impossible task. It led inevitably to bogging down in an attempt at thought control which, as we shall see, has done great harm to our real security interests, has deflected untold energies from defense against the Communists themselves and has brought the whole system into deserved opprobrium.

Those who need to be guarded against are members of the Communist party and those who are under the discipline and control of the Communist party, whether registered on the party books or not. To guard against them effectively will take a good deal more skillful work than mere routine FBI interviewing. Furthermore the government ought to be pretty sure of its case before it charges citizens, in or out of government employment, with belonging to this group, since, as I have said, this— certainly in the layman's mind—amounts to a charge of participation in a criminal conspiracy of a peculiarly opprobrious nature. When the government does so, it ought to be required to prove its charge and present its witnesses before the accused and his judges. It will be said that this will uncover agents and cause people to refuse to give information. As for the latter, we can well do without the tales of those who are not willing to repeat them to the accused. This second-hand storytelling is, at best, unreliable, and as the basis of destroying the reputation, standing, and livelihood of free citizens is intolerable. Uncovering secret agents engaged in protecting us against espionage and sabotage is a serious matter. But it is within the control of the government and will not be lightly done. The decision involves weighing the harm to counterespionage work which comes from the disclosure against the good resulting from the apprehension and removal of the spy or saboteur. Sometimes the government wishes to arrest and try those suspected, sometimes to keep them under watch, in the hope of discovering accomplices. The same weighing of interests is necessary in the case of those suspected of being under Communist discipline and control, and hence potential spies or saboteurs. On the one side is the setback to police work; on the other, the vital importance that in a charge of this moment, the testimony be given in the presence of, and subject to the cross-examination of, the accused, whose whole reputation and livelihood depend upon the outcome. Furthermore, the government would not have to choose one alternative or the other. It could if it was doubtful of its suspicions, or wished to wait until the agent's task was completed, transfer the suspect to harmless work and continue the observation. But to assume, as it is not uncommon for police to do, that the suspect is guilty and does not deserve this protection is to assume away the liberties of the citizen.

The whole effort to penetrate and police the minds and thoughts of employees and prospective employees should be swept out of the security procedures. It is futile and harmful; and when conducted by persons trained in police methods, is usually ludicrous. Insofar as an employee's intellectual experience has relevancy, it is to the suitability of the individual for his employment. For a quarter of a century before security became a by-word, the Foreign Service of the United States carefully and painstakingly selected its personnel from among candidates applying, by inquiry into their backgrounds and by examinations, written and oral, relying on the judgment of its own staff. It would be too much to say that the system always selected the best men. Some, through its own processes, were dropped or dismissed for various reasons in the interest of the service. But, as Mr. George Kennan has written, "The system did not work badly. During the quarter-century that the writer was actively associated with the Foreign Service, something in the neighborhood of three thousand officers must have been employed in it at one time or another; yet he can recall none that was ever discovered to have been disloyal to the country while serving in this capacity, and none that was ever blackmailed by a foreign government."[22] My own experience with the Foreign Service, though only half as long as Mr. Kennan's, accords with his.

The point which this underlines is that, if the investigation and selection of personnel is done conscientiously by persons who know the work for which they are being selected, they will select people who have the qualities

[22] George F. Kennan, "The Future of Our Professional Diplomacy," *Foreign Affairs,* Vol. 33, No. 4, July, 1955, pp. 566, 581.

which make for security. "For example," writes Professor Chafee, "our building inspectors ought to have some architectural training; and the censorship of plays will vary enormously, accordingly as it is exercised by a student of literature or by a police official who has devoted his best years to the suppression of burglars and the regulation of motor traffic."[23] The procedures for selecting and governing the Foreign Service can be, should be, and to a large extent are being, extended to all employees of the Department of State.

Of course, those responsible for the work of government must have scope and discretion in selecting employees in whom they have confidence, and they cannot be required, as a matter of administrative common sense, to establish lack of confidence through the equivalent of a lawsuit. If something turns up to the discredit of a man, they should hear what he has to say about it before coming to a decision. And this requires informal administrative hearings. But it should not include charging him with disloyalty or with thinking thoughts which some handbook declares are not thought by "normal" or "right-thinking" Americans. Every interest of the government and of the individual can be safeguarded if the atmosphere is one of calmness and confidence and fairness. The interest of neither can be served by men obsessed by security, or fear of spies, or fear of criticism.

[23] Zechariah Chafee, Jr., *Free Speech in the United States* (Harvard University Press, Cambridge, 1941), p. 521.

5. THE INEVITABLE RESULTS OF THE SECURITY PROGRAM.

In time, a system of administrative justice carried on as the security programs have been will cause one of two results. It will corrupt our sense of justice, or it will destroy confidence in the justice of the system. I am inclined to think that at the present both results are occurring among different groups of people in this country.

The larger and less thoughtful group is being led to the conclusion that to charge a person with disloyalty raises a presumption of guilt. "Where there is smoke," they say, "there is fire." From this presumption of guilt flows the reversal of values and sense of justice laboriously developed by a free people. Attorney General Brownell elucidates the process in an interview entitled, "Shall Doors Be Opened to Spies and Subversives?";[24] to which the answer would seem obvious. First comes the presumption of great danger to the government in every case:

Q. Is it a question of the number who are found to be in the security-risk category, or is it a question of the damage that can be done by the few?

A. Well, one Klaus Fuchs is enough, isn't it?[25]

Surely, and so is one murderer, one kidnaper, one

[24] Reprinted from *U. S. News & World Report*, an independent weekly news magazine published at Washington. Copyright 1955, United States News Publishing Corporation. April 29, 1955, p. 54.
[25] *Ibid.*

demagogue who undermines the principles, the restraints on the state upon which individual liberty and dignity depend. The issue is not whether one Klaus Fuchs is enough. It is whether a citizen is to be regarded as a potential or actual traitor on the reported word of an informer. For when the charge of disloyalty has been made, the informer becomes the dominating figure, anonymous, speaking from off stage through an intermediary, surrounded by every protection and consideration.

Q. You give him [the accused] all the information, but not the source, is that it?

A. We are not always able to give him the sources. Of course, in certain cases the Communists would like to know what those sources are, because, if they can once spot the confidential informants of the Government, they've won a large part of their battle against our national security. . . .[26]

The charge rests upon alleged information given by informers. They are its sources. Who these sources are, how reliable, how motivated is, of course, information vital to defense and also to final judgment. But neither the accused nor his judges may have this information. It follows that the reliability of the witness and the truth of his testimony has to be left to the F.B.I. The Attorney General says:

[26] *Ibid.*, p. 56.

The FBI seeks to corroborate the information supplied by
the informant and always furnishes information in its reports
reflecting upon the reliability of the informant. In the event
there is no information bearing upon the reliability of the
informant, this fact is shown in order that proper weight can
be afforded the information by those engaged in the adjudi-
cating process.[27]

What is the proper weight to be attached to information given by a witness about whose reliability nothing
is known and who is not present for cross-examination,
the Attorney General does not say, but he does assure
us of the utmost good faith with which the government
has dealt with informants:

Q. How does the number who have been disclosed to
public view and have been in the papers as informers com-
pare with those who have not ever been disclosed—which
number is the larger?

A. It's a comparatively small proportion that ever becomes
known.

Q. So that there is a large number who have not received
publicity or limelight through the giving of information?

A. I'd say an overwhelming percentage.

Q. And the FBI has kept faith with those people?

A. In every case.[28]

[27] *Ibid.*
[28] *Ibid.*

The government's solicitude seems to be exhausted by the informants. Its own employees or advisers come in for rather brusque treatment as the Attorney General describes it:

Q. Do you believe that employment in the Government is a right or is it a matter of discretion on the part of the Government as to who shall remain in its employ?

A. President Eisenhower has said many times that there is no right to work for the Government—it is a privilege, and this position has been accepted since the earliest days of our republic. This privilege carries certain obligations. One of the obligations is that you have to protect your Government's secrets. Likewise, those responsible to the people have an obligation to delegate public duties only to those worthy of complete confidence.

Q. How, then, can it be said under the Constitution a man has a right to be confronted by his accusers at all times? There has lately been a lot of agitation about that—

A. That is correct when you are talking about constitutional safeguards which apply to criminal proceedings.

Q. Do you regard being dismissed from the Government as a penalty or punishment similar to punishment administered for a crime?

A. No, and it never has been so regarded. . . .

Q. What is there to the argument that the stigma which attaches to an employee who is dismissed for incompetence is as nothing compared to the stigma of his having been dismissed for security reasons?

A. Of course every discharge carries some stigma; a doctor who is discharged for professional malpractice would have a stigma attached to his name for all time to come. The same would be true of an employee dismissed for bribery or acts of immorality, as I suggested earlier.

But I would point this out, first, that the fact that you work for the Government does not give you special rights which render you immune from charges. The procedures are set up to give the maximum protection which can be devised consistent with national security.[29]

Not only does the Attorney General conclude that the present procedure is the best that can be devised consistent with the national security, but he thinks also that anyone who suggests otherwise is a Communist, a dupe of Communists, or ignorant of the problem:

Q. Now, if this present procedure is reversed, will that make it easier for spies and saboteurs?

A. It will make it extremely difficult if not almost impossible to dismiss security risks. That, in turn, will make it easier for Communist agents to maintain or develop contacts within the Government. Shall we open the doors to spies and subversives?

Q. Do you think the people who are arguing for these so-called technical changes are doing so without an awareness of the dangers?

A. One group represents the Communist conspiracy, their

[29] *Ibid.*, p. 58.

apologists and dupes. The other represents sincere persons who have never been confronted with the awesome public responsibility for internal security and who do not know the hard facts. It is the Communist, however, who is most vigorously trying to destroy security procedures. There's no doubt that this is part of their current program in this country, to destroy the informant system of the FBI.[30]

The Attorney General's attitude is unhappily typical of the authoritarian mind at all times and places. If the state is faced with internal danger of any sort, the response lies in repression and the secret police. It is thought that dangers rooted in ideas and ideologies can be repressed as burglars are repressed. If burglars are shown to enter more often through back doors and side doors than through front doors, then arrest all who enter through back and side doors. But, one protests, this will result in the arrest principally of innocent householders. The answer recalls us sternly to the path of duty. Shall we open the doors to burglars? Those who suggest this either do not understand the problem and the danger, or they are burglars, or their apologists and dupes.

The authoritarian mind is not interested in a calculation of the cost of repression, or in an appraisal of its effectiveness. Least of all is it concerned with the effect of repression upon the community which employs it. "But," says Mr. George Kennan.

[30] *Ibid.*

the subjective emotional stresses and temptations to which we are exposed in our attempt to deal with this domestic problem . . . represent a danger within ourselves—a danger that something may occur in our own minds and souls which will make us no longer like the persons by whose efforts this republic was founded and held together, but rather like the representatives of that very power we are trying to combat: intolerant, secretive, suspicious, cruel, and terrified of internal dissension because we have lost our own belief in ourselves and in the power of our ideals. The worst thing that our Communists could do to us, and the thing we have most to fear from their activities, is that we should become like them.[31]

"The greatest dangers to liberty," said Mr. Justice Brandeis, "lurk in insidious encroachment by men of zeal, well-meaning but without understanding."[32]

Such is the attitude toward the present security practices of the smaller, but more thoughtful, and in the long run, the more influential group in the country. And with it goes disbelief that the system's results are correct and just. Among this group only the merest handful, for instance, believe that either Dr. Oppenheimer or Mr. Davies are security risks of any sort whatever. Despite the extent to which the government pinned its prestige to these decisions, Dr. Oppenheimer has been reconfirmed

[31] George F. Kennan, "Where Do You Stand on Communism?" *New York Times Magazine*, May 27, 1951, pp. 7, 53.
[32] *Olmstead v. United States*, 277 U.S. 438, 479 (1928).

as Director of the Institute for Advanced Study at Princeton (of which Mr. Strauss, Chairman of the Atomic Energy Commission and who decided against him, is Chairman). And of the Davies decision Mr. James Reston wrote in the *New York Times* (November 10, 1954): "Accordingly, the basic question is not whether Mr. Dulles was right or whether Mr. Davies was right [on matters of foreign policy]. Nobody can have a judgment on that unless he reads the whole record. The question is whether the security regulations are right, and there is reason for saying that even Mr. Dulles has his doubts on that score."

Among this group, whose opinion will carry increasing weight, these cases brought loss of confidence in the security system itself, rather than in its victims. The government has done a grave disservice to the undoubted interest in an effective and just system of security.

The damage the government has done has affected not merely the protective aspect of security, the police aspect of attempting to discover and then to remove, or not to employ, the disloyal or untrustworthy. This important endeavor, as we have seen, has been impeded by the unnecessarily large numbers of people with whom it has concerned itself and by the lack of confidence in the system which the methods employed have engendered. The damage done has been far greater. It has seriously impaired most essential positive requirements of national

security—the morale and effectiveness of two professional groups upon whom the government and all of us
must greatly rely—the scientific and the State Depart-
ment-Foreign Service group. The contribution of these
men in their respective fields is of critical importance. It
lies in the forefront of the determination of our national
fortunes. This is perhaps the ironical reason why the
damage should have been done pre-eminently to them.

The fate and state of the scientists under the security
program of the past five years is the subject of the entire
special issue of the *Bulletin of the Atomic Scientists* of
April, 1955, Volume XI, No. 4. It is grim reading. I
choose a few paragraphs from the introductory article by
the special editor of this issue, because through its strict
restraint and understatement comes even more clearly
the realization of what we are doing to ourselves.

The effect on science as such is difficult to assess. It is impossible even for a scientist of genius to assess a lost opportunity of which he was unaware. The freedom of science is so
important to its progress just because it allows the accidental
to occur. Discovery of scientific truth is too unpredictable to
allow anyone to say exactly what has been lost to American
science through the unnecessary restriction of communication and the distraction and harassment generated by a security system made more extreme than realism requires, from
an obsession with loyalty. A small number of senior scientists
and some outstanding younger scientists have apparently

refused to work in fields dominated by the security procedures. A large number have been prevented from working in
these fields, and an even larger group, consisting mainly of
younger men of high quality, who are both cleared and willing to work under security procedures, feel harried and constricted in working under what they consider conditions of
unjustifiable discrimination, diminution of their freedom,
and lack of esteem for the dignity of science.

Both scientists and generals of great practical experience
have asserted that if the postwar security provisions had obtained during the war, it would not have been possible to
have accomplished anything approximating the great successes of wartime scientific research.

. . . .

. . . It was criteria of loyalty which excluded Professors
Szilard, Wigner, von Neumann, Franck, Weisskopf, Meitner
and the late Enrico Fermi from the scientific communities
in their own countries. The effects of this exclusion and its
benefits for science in America are known to all. Yet, in a
certainly more conscientious and ostensibly more rational
way, the United States government is blocking the boundaries
of the scientific community, refusing research grants, denying
visas, suspending scientists, and denying fellowships on criteria which, although far less brutal, are almost as unrealistic
and as irrelevant to truth, national security, or welfare as the
Nazi and Fascist criteria.

While, on the one hand, the National Science Foundation,
the Atomic Energy Commission, and the U.S. Public Health
Service are doing all they can to attract the best young minds

to science, and to provide them with the means for prosecuting their research, the security-loyalty policies of the government are unwittingly undoing the government's own work by making the scientific career less attractive and more worrisome and distracting than it must be if creativity in scientific discovery is to be fostered.[33]

The damage which has been done in the Department of State is equally great. Here it is perhaps more possible to put one's finger on the incidence of the evil. The first, I think, is the establishment since 1952 of a dual authority in the Department: One, under the Secretary, deals directly with foreign policy; another, under the Administrator of the Bureau of Inspection, Security and Consular Affairs, deals indirectly but powerfully with foreign policy through its power over the personnel of the Department derived from the control of security. Theoretically this second authority is subordinate to the Secretary. But Professor Hans Morgenthau has pointed out that "As in fully developed totalitarian systems the power of the secret police is in good measure the reflection of the political power of its head. . . ."[34] By this test it is not too much to say that this second authority in the administration of the security program is not responsive

[33] Edward Shils, "Security and Science Sacrificed to Loyalty," *Bulletin of the Atomic Scientists*, Vol. XI, Number 4, April, 1955, pp. 106, 108-109.

[34] Hans J. Morgenthau, *op. cit.*, p. 138.

to the Secretary, or even to the Executive branch, but to individuals in Congress.

As a maker and executor of foreign policy, whatever the appearances, the Secretary is not an individual performer. He is part of an institution, another essential part of which is the personnel of the Department of State and the Foreign Service, from which flow to him his information and his initial analysis of problems and recommendations for dealing with them. The power to break these men, as every totalitarian regime has discovered, is power at the center. When it is exercised under an obsession with security, with fear of the unconventional, the diverse point of view, it brings stagnation and timidity.

Couple with this the identification of disloyalty with participation by Foreign Service officers in events which have been under intense political attack and the demoralization of the personnel serving under the Secretary of State is made certain. Five of our senior diplomats, with the insight of their long experience, have described this demoralization.

The conclusion has become inescapable, for instance, that a Foreign Service officer who reports on persons and events to the very best of his ability and who makes recommendations which at the time he conscientiously believes to be in the interest of the United States may subsequently find his loyalty and integrity challenged and may even be forced out of the service and discredited forever as a private citizen after many years of distinguished service. A premium therefore has been put upon reporting and upon recommendations which are ambiguously stated or so cautiously set forth as to be deceiving.

When any such tendency begins its insidious work it is not long before accuracy and initiative have been sacrificed to acceptability and conformity. The ultimate result is a threat to national security. In this connection the history of the Nazi and Fascist foreign services before the Second World War is pertinent.

The forces which are working for conformity from the outside are being reinforced by the present administrative set-up within the Department of State which subordinates normal personnel administration to considerations of security.

It is obvious, of course, that candidates for the Foreign Service should be carefully investigated before appointment and that their work should at all times be under the exacting scrutiny of their professional superiors. But when initial investigation attaches undue importance to such factors as even a temporary departure from conservative political and economic views, casual association with persons holding views not currently in fashion or subscription to a periodical labeled as "liberal"; when subsequent investigation is carried to the point of delaying a promotion list for a year and routine transfers from one post to another; when investigations of individual officers must be kept up to date to within ninety days; when an easy path has been opened to even the anonymous informer; and when the results of these investigations are evaluated not by persons experienced in the Foreign Service or even acquainted at firsthand with conditions abroad, but by persons of quite different experience, it is relevant to inquire whether we are not laying the foundations of a Foreign Service competent to serve a totalitarian government rather than the Government of the United States as we have heretofore known it.[35]

Americans know little of the actual results of what has been done because they rarely see our Foreign Service in action as they see internal revenue agents or county agents of the Department of Agriculture. Here is one observer's report of the state of this service, which is not our eyes and ears abroad but upon whose common sense and wise advice hang the gravest issues of our national future:

This disintegration of the Foreign Service of the United States is better known abroad than it is at home. The governments and public opinion of foreign countries have seen with amazement officials, of whose competence and loyalty they have had tangible evidence, investigated, dismissed, or forced to resign as security risks. Continuous contacts with our representatives abroad provide them with unmistakable evidence of the diminution of their professional competence. This writer who has recently had occasion to ask officials, political leaders, and journalists of European countries what

[35] Letter of January 14, 1954, from Norman Armour, Robert Woods Bliss, Joseph C. Grew, William Phillips and G. Howland Shaw, *New York Times*, January 17, 1954.

they think of the Foreign Service of the United States has been shocked and dismayed by the instances of individual incompetence reported to him, by the invidious comparisons with times past, and by the condescension and contempt to be found at every turn.[36]

6. HOW FAR ARE SECURITY PROCEDURES AFFECTING THE LIVES OF AMERICAN CITIZENS?

The point at which the state, in the first instance, asserted new powers and new methods was in dealing with its employees—a relationship which is always peculiarly revealing. As its methods became more arbitrary and departed further from historic conceptions, they were justified by claims familiar in societies where the individual is thought to depend for his status and position upon the favor of the state. President Eisenhower stated at his press conference of December 2, 1953, that employment in the federal government is not a right of citizenship but a privilege.[37] He said this not in response to any claim that citizens had a right to be employed by the government or because of any formidable impediment in the way of discharging them if the need for their work ended or if they were unsuitable for it. It was said in defense of procedures for detecting and removing persons described as "risks." The idea was that here procedures could be less exacting because the em-

[36] Hans J. Morgenthau, op. cit., p. 140.
[37] See Washington Post, December 3, 1953.

ployees were enjoying a favor or privilege rather than standing on a right.

This conception deserves examination for the light it throws on the present relationship between the individual and the state. Does it succeed in establishing federal employees as a small group, different from the rest of us, whose livelihood rests upon a privilege which can properly be withdrawn by whatever method seems good to the state? I do not think so. I think rather that each of us will find that to an important degree his daily life is based upon what he thinks of as a right, but which some official might, quite as easily as in the case of federal employees, call a privilege and claim the power to withdraw.

Former Senator Harry Cain points out that the same procedures, used to deprive federal employees of the privilege of working for the federal government, also govern the employees of private industries working on certain types of contracts with the government. He states that directly or indirectly they affect the livelihood of twenty million Americans.[38]

Professor Ralph S. Brown, Jr., dealing with this question, concludes:

If we combine our estimates of the numbers of employees exposed to some existing loyalty or security test, this is the result:

[38] The Honorable Harry P. Cain, "Strong in Their Pride and Free," *op. cit.*, p. 16.

	(in thousands)
Professions, including teachers	1,600
Managers	300
Government and military	7,200
Extractive industry	...
Manufacturing, construction, transport, utilities	3,500
Trade, service, finance	...
Agriculture	...
	Total....12,600

Taking the total labor force at around 62,000,000, this means that one person out of five, as a condition of his employment, has taken a test oath, or completed a loyalty statement, or achieved official clearance, or survived some undefined private scrutiny.[39]

If we include the dependents of these persons, as I assume Senator Cain does in his estimate, the total must be considerably higher than the Senator's figures. The matter begins to look a good deal more serious when one-eighth to one-fifth of our people live by a privilege which the state can revoke. But this is only the beginning of the matter.

Not long ago I received my automobile license plates for 1955. They came in a large envelope, on the back of which was printed:

[39] Ralph S. Brown, Jr., "Loyalty-Security Measures and Employment Opportunities," *Bulletin of the Atomic Scientists*, Vol. XI, Number 4, April, 1955, pp. 113, 117.

Mr. Motorist!

Your driver's permit is only a *Privilege*. It is not a *Right*....

The authorities then admonished me, quite properly, to drive at safe speeds. They did not say anything about being a "risk" in the President's sense of the word. But recently in the same city one William Shonick ran into this kind of trouble.

Mr. Shonick was a dealer in secondhand pianos. He applied, as he was required to, for a renewal of his license as a secondhand dealer. This license was "only a privilege" for which he had to qualify as I did for my driver's license. His license was denied "on a finding that he is 'under Communist discipline.' " He had previously lost a job as a teacher for the same reason. On appeal, the examiner came to the conclusion that there was evidence of Communist sympathies which Shonick, by pleading the Fifth Amendment, refused to rebut. Nevertheless, the examiner recommended that the license be renewed, "I find," he said, "that while appellant is not in the strict and inclusive sense of the term a person of good character, his character is sufficiently good within the meaning of Article I, Section 5, Police Regulations to require the renewal of his license as a secondhand dealer."[40]

So the question is, how good is "sufficiently good" to give one the character one needs to get or keep the license

[40] "Preliminary Report of Hearing" on appeal of William Shonick, D.C. Board of Appeals and Review, Docket No. 8, p. 12.

one has to have to earn one's living? Who is going to decide, and under what safeguards?

We lawyers have to pass a character test to get our licenses to practice, although we call them not licenses, but certificates of admission to the bar. Before the Eighty-fourth Congress are two companion bills, S.2326, introduced by Senator Eastland of Mississippi, and H.R. 7070, introduced by Representative Rodino of New Jersey. The titles of these bills describe them as follows: "To require any attorney at law practicing before a Federal court, or appearing before a congressional committee as counsel for a witness testifying before such committee, or appearing as counsel before any department or agency in the Executive branch of the Government of the United States, to file a non-Communist affidavit."

In the city where I live good character or reputation is needed for licenses as: physicians, dentists, dental hygienists, registered nurses, optometrists, pharmacists, podiatrists, veterinarians, certified public accountants, architects, barbers and barber apprentices, master plumbers and gas fitters, steam and operating engineers, professional engineers, real-estate and business-chance brokers and salesmen, insurance brokers and salesmen, sellers of alcoholic beverages, operators of employment agencies, massage establishments, Turkish baths, bowling alleys, mechanical amusement machines, poolrooms, and nursing and convalescent homes, guides, dealers in dangerous weapons, private detectives, fortunetellers, managers of lodging, rooming and boardinghouses, undertakers, drivers of busses, taxicabs, streetcars, ambulances and hearses, solicitors, parking-lot attendants, secondhand dealers and beggars.

And we still are not at the end of the matter. One needs a license to operate a busline, railroad, or airline; to be a pilot of any of these conveyances; to operate a radio or television station; to be a seaman; for a boat; to build a house; to use the second-class mail; to get married; to hold a parade or outdoor meeting; to travel abroad. The list could be drawn out indefinitely. Today some of the licenses or permits depend upon security clearance. The same reasons could be extended to require it in all.

The lives of nearly all of us in this complicated age depend on privileges which the state may grant or refuse and which are not "rights of citizenship." Indeed, rights of citizenship would not get us very far in our daily lives. Freedom is preserved not by drawing distinctions between rights and privileges, but by our demanding and maintaining rights in privileges. In the *National Gazette* of March 29, 1792, James Madison made clear his views on this point:

> In its larger and juster meaning, it [the term "property"] embraces every thing to which a man may attach a value and have a right; and *which leaves to every one else the like ad-*

vantage. In the former sense, a man's land, or merchandise, or money is called his property. In the latter sense, a man has property in his opinions and the free communication of them. He has a property of peculiar value in his religious opinions, and in the profession and practice dictated by them. He has property very dear to him in the safety and liberty of his person. He has an equal property in the free use of his faculties and free choice of the objects on which to employ them. In a word, as a man is said to have a right to his property, he may be equally said to have a property in his rights.[41]

There is very little left of our fighting faith in the dignity and worth of the individual if all of us in one way or another become supplicants for the favors of the state. Our dependence may be on a license to earn our living, or to build our house, or to drive our car, or to go outside the country for any purpose. But, if the license, in turn, depends on the dossier of a secret police which neither we nor the deciding official may see, but of which the latter may obtain an "evaluated summary," then we have abandoned a fundamental requisite of a free people; then the relationship between the individual and the state is badly and dangerously weighted in favor of the state. This is a very present and lively danger. It confronts not merely civil servants. It already is affecting millions of employees and officers in private industry. It can easily affect any one of us.

[41] *The Complete Madison* (Harper & Brothers, Padover Ed., New York, 1953), p. 267.

In our concern over the danger from the Communist conspiracy we have been driven, as I have already said, to a search for an illusion, the illusion of complete security. This is not and never has been attainable; and the attempt to approximate it, to push to the utmost precautions against harm from subversive influences, has done far more damage than good to our real security and has made deep inroads in the practice of our faith—and hence in our faith—in the dignity and worth of the individual.

It is essential to the survival and revival of freedom in America and of the respect which other free peoples in the world hold for America that we regain our confidence in one another here at home and in the principles of government and justice which express that confidence. This is essential also if we are to achieve that degree of security against those bent on subversion and harm to us which is practically possible. For this security can be achieved only in a different atmosphere than now exists —in an atmosphere in which an obsession with security is replaced by a passion for liberty and justice, an atmosphere in which officials are both disciplined and free to concentrate their efforts upon those who may realistically be regarded as under the control of a foreign state and acting in its interests.

7

The State and the Individual—

A Party Position

"The most fundamental reform, then, is a reform in fundamental point of view. The most urgent reform is a reform of perspective in the direction of greater realism and common sense. The threat of espionage must be assessed for what it is, and countermeasures taken by security and counterintelligence. The threat of subversion must also be assessed for what it is worth at present—and that is very little—and adequate surveillance by counterintelligence methods maintained. The inflation of the problems of loyalty and security and their fusion must be reversed.

"One of the conditions of this reversal is the restoration of the self-confidence and common sense of the moderate element in our political leadership. For several years the moderate, the respectable, and serious elements in our political élite have allowed themselves to be bullied and misled by a very small minority of vociferous demagogues and their febrile popular following. The moderates, fearing that they were perhaps out of touch with the true course of opinion, accepted the leadership, the perspective, and the standards of a handful of men who claimed to speak for the populace. Nothing could have been less justified or more unwise.

"The time has now come for these errors of judgment and political tactics to be rectified. Let the respectable moderates, the true liberals in both parties, take the lead in the rediscovery of the obviously sensible thing to do about security—to make secure what needs to be secure for purposes of national military strength—and let all else go free. They will be surprised to discern the calming effects this will have on American opinion and how much assent they will find for the policy. They will be remembered for years to come for their reinstatement of America's good name in the world, and they will have earned the appreciation of all who prize freedom and America's embodiment of it."[1]

I cannot do better than to adopt Professor Shils's words. This "reform in fundamental point of view" calls, as he sees it, for leadership which transcends party, for the leadership of the moderate element, the true liberals in both parties. It does indeed; and nothing would be more welcome. But Democrats must look first to their responsibilities in their own ranks.

[1] Edward Shils, "Security and Science Sacrificed to Loyalty," *op. cit.*, p. 130.

We cannot blink the fact that a heavy burden of responsibility lies upon us. Our inheritance, the inheritance from Jefferson and the founders of our party, was a rich and glorious one. The use we have made of it in our own time cannot be a matter of pride. One who admits fault and error is not called upon to prove them, though there is material enough in the prosecutions under the Espionage Act of 1917, during and after the First World War, in the implications of guilt by association in the Alien Registration Act of 1940, in some of the conceptions and the administration of the Loyalty Order of 1947 and the establishment of the Attorney General's list, in the Internal Security Act of 1950, and the Immigration Act of 1952. Not that these were party measures. Indeed President Truman protested against the Internal Security bill by his stirring special message of August 8, 1950, on "preserving our basic liberties," and vetoed the bill when it was passed, as he did the Immigration Act also. So, as has been said, the security measures were not party measures; they had strong bipartisan and popular support. But the Administration of them was Democratic administration and the responsibility for leadership lay in the Democratic party, the party in power.

The error in all these instances lay in departure from principle. "Temporary deviations from fundamental principles," wrote Madison, "are always more or less dangerous. When the first pretext fails, those who become interested in prolonging the evil will rarely be at a loss for other pretexts."[2] The principles which were here disregarded were among the most fundamental we have ever held. The reasons for departing from them, the dangers envisaged, were honestly conceived and understandable enough. But the price to be paid was both inevitable and high.

What has been done is done. We should learn from it and not dissipate energies in mourning it. The challenge of the future is to accept the responsibility for leading the return to principle, to the reform in fundamental point of view. It is one thing to write these words; it is quite another for a political party led, and necessarily led, by men engaged in the practicalities of the struggle for the control of government to act on them.

Politicians do not become such or become successful by throwing themselves away on forlorn causes or espousing views unpalatable to their constituents. So it is not enough to conclude that a course is right to make it politically feasible. Politics is the art of the possible. Is "the reform in fundamental point of view," which we have been considering, is the rekindling of the American faith in the dignity and worth of the individual unpalatable to the American voter, and particularly to those

[2] Letter to John Brown (Kentucky), August 23, 1785, *Writings of James Madison* (J. B. Lippincott & Co., Philadelphia, 1865), Vol. I, pp. 177, 183.

groups of voters from which the Democratic party draws its support?

There is good reason to suppose that it is not unpalatable. There is good reason to suppose that the American people are not suffering from an anxiety neurosis over the internal Communist threat, that they are ready and willing to take a common-sense view of this whole matter if the truth is intelligently presented to them, and that the tendencies which lead to tolerance of diverse views, to faith in the beliefs underlying the Bill of Rights, to the basic concepts which make a democracy work are growing stronger, not weaker. There is a basis, which does not rest on wishful thinking, for believing that, given sensible and unfrightened leadership, the future in America lies with the great tradition of individual freedom and dignity, and not with a conformity induced by fear and coercion.

Each person has his own method of determining what the American people are thinking and believing. It may come from talking with other people—taxi drivers, neighbors, associates in business or shop, church, lodge, or club—or from the newspapers, radio, or television. But Professor Samuel A. Stouffer of Harvard University went about it in a more orderly and considered way. With funds and staff provided for the purpose, adopting the modern methods of sample polling under the guidance of Mr. Elmo Roper, he and his associates undertook to find out current attitudes, ideas, and the direction of movement of American thought on these very matters we have been discussing. He reports his conclusions and data in *Communism, Conformity, and Civil Liberties*, subtitled "A Cross-section of the Nation Speaks Its Mind."[3] Practitioners of the art of politics would do well to heed it.

To heed it does not mean that one accepts it as a "scientific" ascertainment of truth. I doubt that its author would claim that. He concedes that a different survey might produce results differing considerably. And one must remember, too, that opinions differ not only in content but in the intensity with which they are held, and hence in the effect which they may have on others. But, as an indication of a trend, which certainly seems to be in accord with other evidence of a movement in public opinion, it points up and sharpens understanding of some of the forces and factors which are making for the change.

Summarizing the broad conclusion based on analysis of the polling material, Professor Stouffer writes:

We have found no evidence that the country as a whole is suffering from quivering fear or from an anxiety neurosis about the internal Communist threat. If there is a sickness, the clinical symptoms are more like dietary deficiency.

People have a table fare of vague and distorted information

[3] Doubleday & Company, Inc., New York, 1955.

about the Communist danger. They exaggerate present-day conversions of Americans to Communism and they have little awareness, let alone concern, about many of the harmful counteractions to such dangers as do exist.

If a more balanced and palatable diet of information and education were to be made available, what does the study show about the prospects of acceptance?

Although anticipating that some interpreters of the American scene may disagree, the author offers his considered judgment that the prospects, on balance, should be good.[4]

In spite of the past five years of hammering on the fear of Communist subversion, less than 1 per cent of those questioned considered it their chief source of concern.[5] Americans are not in a hysterical frame of mind. Moreover—and perhaps this is the most significant conclusion of the study—

Great social, economic, and technological forces are working on the side of exposing ever larger proportions of our population to the idea that "people are different from me, with different systems of values, and they can be good people, too." This would seem to be a necessary condition to tolerance, but not the only condition. It should be a first step to the recognition that it is good for a country both to respect the civil rights of people whose ideas challenge cherished traditions and to preserve a free market place of ideas even if they seem dangerous. And that the country can and must

[4] *Ibid.*, p. 220.
[5] *Ibid.*, p. 59.

do this, while still standing firm against its enemies from within and without. In this book we have seen some of these great forces at work.[6]

These forces could cause movement in either direction, toward tolerance or toward conformity, and, in part, they do both—but the significant fact is that in the present American environment they are working for tolerance.[7] The forces are the almost revolutionary changes of the level of education within two generations, the mobility of the population by which increasing numbers, chiefly the young, find themselves in new environments, with new values and points of view, and the phenomenal growth of communications by which people learn and have a real feel of other people, different from themselves, with different ideas but common purposes. To a large extent these forces affect most importantly the groups among the electorate of which the politicians with an eye to the future must be most keenly aware, and it is among these that the tendencies making for tolerance of nonconformity is high and highest.

The young—those under thirty—have had more education than their elders and have also a higher degree of tolerance, the degree progressing with the amount of education. Important, also, is the fact that in this group the less tolerant minority is small. Among the older group the study brings out that, while the percentage of

[6] *Ibid.*, pp. 220-221.
[7] *Ibid.*, Chapter Nine.

those more tolerant of nonconformity is smaller than among the young, it, also, progresses with the amount of education. Factors making for a more tolerant electorate are education and the increased participation of the younger element of the population in politics.[8]

The sampling was, also, directed to bringing out a comparison of the attitudes of civic leaders with those of a cross-section of the population.[9] Civic leaders included mayors, heads of schools and library boards, chairmen of political party central committees, presidents of Chambers of Commerce and labor unions, of patriotic organizations, community chests and bar associations, women's clubs and parent-teacher associations, and newspaper publishers.

The results of the testing are instructive. Not only is the proportion of the more tolerant among civic leaders preponderant, but it is substantially higher than the figures for the cross-section of their own communities. The trend of leadership in the localities is in the right direction—moreover, responses to specific questions show discrimination. While civic leaders would not approve of an admitted Communist working in a defense plant (93 per cent), or teaching in a high school (89 per cent), a majority (51 per cent) would favor letting him speak in their communities. If the person concerned has had his loyalty questioned, but swears he is not a Communist,

[8] *Ibid.*, Chapter Four.
[9] *Ibid.*, Chapter Two.

87 per cent would favor letting him speak (and the percentage holding this view among both presidents of Chambers of Commerce and newspaper publishers exceeds the average), 80 per cent would let him teach in a high school and 81 per cent in a college, 82 per cent would let him work in a defense plant, 93 per cent in a store, 91 per cent as a radio singer. "What," asks Professor Stouffer, "does this mean?" In his opinion it means "that the community leaders, being especially responsible and thoughtful citizens, are more likely than the rank and file to give a sober second thought to the dangers involved in denying civil liberties to those whose views they dislike."[10]

For the politician another significant conclusion of the study is that the incidence of tolerance of noncomformists is highest in the areas which for him are the most doubtful. The West leads, then comes the East, followed by the Middle West and the South. The same order held good when the regions were ranked by the degree of education possessed by the groups sampled within them. Furthermore, in all of these areas tolerance of nonconformity is higher in the urban districts than in the rural ones. When the views of those who had had college, high-school, or only grade-school education were compared by regions, the differences were much reduced.[11]

[10] *Ibid.*, p. 27.
[11] *Ibid.*, Chapter Five.

This again stresses the bearing of education upon tolerance of nonconformity and suggests that more rapid
advance is likely to be made where educational opportunities previously lacking are made available.

One final aspect of the study deserves comment. One
of the objects of the tests was to learn what those questioned most feared about Communism.[12] The conclusion
of the author is clear—"More people are bothered about
the possibility that Communists will convert other Americans to Communism than about espionage or possible
sabotage in case of war."[13] The figures are:

> Sabotage 8%
> Espionage 8%
> Conversion and
>   spreading ideas 28%

These replies offer both opportunity and challenge to
the responsible political leaders. What most of these
people fear most about Communism is a quite erroneous
and unfounded fear. For many years the danger of con-
verting Americans to Communism has declined to the
point of being negligible. The attempts to penetrate labor
unions and other organizations have been unmasked.
The real purpose of the Communist party as an agent of
Soviet policy has been demonstrated again and again.
Communism has no roots in the United States, no allure

[12] *Ibid.*, Chapter Seven.
[13] *Ibid.*, p. 186.

for American citizens. As pointed out in the preceding chapter, espionage and sabotage can be dealt with by counterintelligence methods. They cannot be dealt with by security and loyalty programs. Here, then, is a fertile field for political education and leadership, in the true traditions of our party and nation.

It would be a familiar field to Thomas Jefferson. If he were told that Americans feared Communists among them, because they might win converts to subvert our institutions, he would reply as he did in the first inaugural address to almost the same fears:

If there be any among us who would wish to dissolve this Union or to change its republican form, let them stand undisturbed as monuments of the safety with which error of opinion may be tolerated where reason is left free to combat it. I know, indeed, that some honest men fear that a republican government cannot be strong; that this government is not strong enough. But would the honest patriot, in full tide of successful experiment, abandon a government which has so far kept us free and firm, on the theoretic and visionary fear that this government, the world's best hope, may by possibility want energy to preserve itself? I trust not. I believe this, on the contrary, the strongest government on earth. I believe it is the only one where every man, at the call of the laws, would fly to the standard of the law, and would meet invasions of the public order as his own personal concern. Sometimes it is said that man cannot be trusted with the government of himself. Can he, then, be trusted with the government of others? Or have we found angels, in the forms of kings to govern him?[14]

And, if he were told—possibly by Attorney General Brownell—that our security rested on the coercive force of secret agents, secret evidence, secret records to protect us against any with "a sympathetic interest in totalitarian ideologies," he would reply with scathing contempt:

Reason and experiment have been indulged, and error has fled before them. It is error alone which needs the support of government. Truth can stand by itself. Subject opinion to coercion: whom will you make your inquisitors? Fallible men; men governed by bad passions, by private as well as public reasons. And why subject it to coercion? To produce uniformity. But is uniformity of opinion desireable? No more than of face and stature. Introduce the bed of Procrustes then, and as there is danger that the large men may beat the small, make us all of a size, by lopping the former and stretching the latter. . . . Is uniformity attainable? Millions of innocent men, women, and children, since the introduction of Christianity, have been burnt, tortured, fined, imprisoned; yet we have not advanced one inch toward uniformity. What has been the effect of coercion? To make one half the world fools, and the other half hypocrites. To support roguery and error all over the earth.[15]

[14] First Inaugural Address, March 4, 1801, *The Writings of Thomas Jefferson* (The Thomas Jefferson Memorial Association, 1903), Vol. III, pp. 317, 319-320.
[15] Thomas Jefferson, *Notes on the State of Virginia* (University of North Carolina Press, William Peden Ed., Chapel Hill, 1955), p. 160.

Professor Stouffer's study will not furnish political leaders with a sense of direction or with convictions of principle, but it gives strong encouragement for the belief that the "reform in fundamental point of view," for which Professor Shils calls, is within the practicalities of politics. For the Democratic party it is very nearly within the necessities of politics. As the coercion for conformity broadens out beyond the employees of government to include the employees of industry, teachers in private and public schools, seamen, dockworkers, and many others, it bears with particular harshness on groups from whom the Democratic party draws support, and who can look only to political action for relief from this oppression. Here and there a well-known scientist, official, or citizen, whose case is publicized in the press, can find friends and sympathizers to lend legal and financial assistance. But the obscure victim of this secret and baffling system is helpless, often suspended from employment, without funds, and with friends falling away. For those whom Lincoln called affectionately "the common people" the only security from this new insecurity lies in a basic change in governmental attitude. For this they will look to their party and their party will do well to provide the leadership in returning to its own basic principles.

There is another pressing necessity for Democratic leadership in this reform. The Democratic party, as we have seen earlier, looks upon government as the whole people organized to do essential jobs, jobs which, in fact, are not being done. It peculiarly needs Executive agencies which are effective, energetic, and imaginative. They cannot do what the party, when in power, will ask of them and be staffed with mere jobholders and officered by colorless conformists, blameless because they have never had the intellectual energy to be anything at all. For Democratic Administrations the skill, the resourcefulness, the innovating energy of these governmental staffs will mean the difference between success and failure in their programs. For a Democratic Administration to have made the botch of the polio vaccine program which has been done by the present Republican created and staffed Department would have destroyed it. Democratic programs are designed to produce results and are judged by them. They are not "experiments in states' rights."

It is this very capacity in executive agencies which the loyalty-security program is destroying. Government service is being made intolerable for intellectuals—eggheads, if you like—who have in the past rendered such brilliant service to Democratic administrations.

Devastating, despairing, and ignorant criticism of public servants and of their effectiveness is in deadly contradiction to our vital need to attract and to hold outstanding qualified people in the public service. It has in it the germs of destruction of all government. No more subtle method of subversion exists and none plays more into the hands of the Communists than the recurrent campaigns of insidious, blanket derogation of public employees as a class. Nor is the situation helped by periodic forays into employee activities by demagogues, whether disguised in the name of national security or in the name of efficiency. It is high time that public servants were taken off the defensive and given recognition for their genuine achievements rather than notoriety for the misdeeds of a few.[16]

What has been written above has a strong utilitarian tinge. This has its important place. Considerations of practicality may tell the political leader that he is not a fool for leading where he wants to lead. They cannot give him his inner fire or tell him where he wants to lead. This comes out of himself and out of his past. If he is to be a real leader of the Democratic party, it comes in a most persistent way out of the traditions of the party and those postulates of policy which he shares with its great leaders. He believes, as they believed, that "the only enterprise that is really private is intellectual enterprise, and upon this depends all other enterprise; the only American habit that can really be called a system is the habit of pluralism and experimentation."[17] And he

[16] O. Glenn Stahl (Executive Vice-Chairman, Interagency Advisory Group, U.S. Civil Service Commission), "Security of Tenure—Career or Sinecure?" *Annals of the American Academy of Political and Social Science*, March, 1954, pp. 45, 51.

[17] Henry Steele Commager, *Freedom, Loyalty, Dissent* (Oxford University Press, New York, 1954), p. 69.

knows that coercion to conform is the death sentence for freedom of the individual mind and spirit; that the sovereignty of the people ends when the government lays down what the people may safely believe.

There is a tendency to become discouraged with party leadership during those periods when the Executive power is not in Democratic hands and when the authority to determine party positions and actions is exercised by Congressional leaders. Then we are accustomed to astute political management, but feel the lack of the authentic touch, of the unifying and inspiring experience of policy seen as a whole, supported by the power to mold the forces of government to make the conception effective. This is not because Congressional leaders are less able or less devoted to party principles than a President or a candidate for the Presidency, but because their function is a more limited and particular one, dealing, as they must, with this or that bill or inquiry, and because the pressures which bear on them are more parochial—not merely in the geographical sense, but from the point of view of subject matter as well. One man may be concentrated on military affairs, another on power development, another on public roads, and so on. It is only when the party is fully in power or is engaged in the attempt to attain it, that the full potentialities of leadership are called forth.

So it is not a cause for discouragement that not more is heard today from Democratic leaders on the fundamental issues and principles with which these last two chapters are concerned. Our wish is by no means the only ground for believing that, when the party position is fully expounded and its forces deployed for a national effort, the authentic and historic voice and doctrine of the Democratic party will point the way to sanity and respect for the rights of the citizen. In the indefinable interplay between leaders and people the molecular forces that in the end make party attitude, or receptiveness to attitude, are steadily at work. The sense of disgust at demagoguery over loyalty and security is manifest. The "sober second thought to the dangers involved in denying civil liberties" even to civil servants, is under way. Already the American sense of fair play is awakened by the most dramatic injustices which come to general attention. The deeper realization of the full scope of the assault which has taken place on the free intellectual enterprise upon which rests all else that we have and are is still to come. That it will come is not inevitable. But the thoughts in innumerable minds have prepared them for a leadership which, if it comes, will unite them into a flood in the true channel of Democratic and American tradition. To bring this about requires from those who understand the need of it effort and a fighting faith; but first it requires that they give heed to that admonition in the Book of Common Prayer, "Lift up your hearts."

8

Epilogue

AS I LOOK ahead, there loom problems and tasks for
our people, which will need for their wise and successful management all the youthful vitality of the
Democratic party of which I have written, all the bold
imaginativeness of its empirical nature, the common
sense of its conservatism, and its broad base among many
different groups with their many interests. These needs
of the future cannot be served by formulae, nor will the
American people entrust their interests to narrow or
doctrinaire leadership. They do not believe that they are,
or have to be—and most certainly they do not want to be
—pawns in the clutch of economic forces. They do not
believe, and evidence plentifully supports them, that our
system of private property is identifiable with the capital-

ism which Marx described, moving relentlessly to cata-
clysm and the impoverishment of the people. The conception and the leadership which will be adequate to
the tasks and command the confidence of the people
must be rooted in their experience and traditions, and
responsive, not to a dominant interest in the world of
property, but to a large number of interrelated interests
of a large number of people. To provide this, I have said
earlier, a party oriented and largely directed by business
and the business point of view seems to me to be handicapped by too constricted a view of what is, from time to
time, necessary and permissible, and by too narrow a
popular base to provide the confidence essential in difficult times.

Since I started this writing we have had a unique
revelation of the functions of government as seen from
the business point of view and of the relation between
business and the Republican party. It is contained in the
reports of the second Hoover Commission. The first
Hoover Commission was, as Mr. Hoover said, "for various reasons unable to deal with policy questions."[1]
These reasons consisted of a majority of the Commission
which was unable to believe that the mandate to review
the efficiency of the organization of the Executive branch

[1] The Honorable Herbert Hoover, "The Work of the Commission
on Reorganization of the Government," address before the National
Industrial Conference Board, May 19, 1955, *Congressional Record*,
June 6, 1955, p. A3960.

extended to reviewing the substance of legislation enacted in the constitutional manner. This, it seemed to us, was a function which the Congress had not delegated to us and surely should not. But that was changed on the second attempt. "This," said former Senator Homer Ferguson with relish, "will give us an opportunity at last to reverse the trend of the last twenty years."[2]

The opportunity was not let slip. Through "task forces" selected personally by Mr. Hoover from the business world, the reports of the Commission speak as uninhibitedly as a child's letter to Santa Claus or the harassed executive on the psychoanalyst's couch. Here is the authentic voice of the Republican party, the voice of the business community. Far more than the good-natured ambivalence of President Eisenhower's "progressive conservatism," these reports state what the business heart and center of the party really wants. One report brought echoes of my childhood when the "Progressives," the "Insurgents," the "Young Turks" in the House and Senate thundered, "There are only three arguments against the proposed parcel post—the Adams Express Company, the American Express Company, and Wells, Fargo & Company." Now there is only one argument, the Railway Express Agency, but it is enough for the Hoover Commission. Away with the parcel post, it says; stop this government competition.

[2] St. Louis Post Dispatch, May 26, 1955, p. 2B.

It cannot all be stopped, Mr. Hoover concedes regretfully—one of few concessions to time and change. "In a few cases, having no hope of completely recovering our national philosophy of life, we recommend that the government competitor be put on a self-supporting basis."[3] But there are not many such moments of weak resignation to the twentieth century. For the most part the clean sweep includes the Army PX, federal medical services, Veterans Administration and Public Health general hospitals, government lending, public water and power development, most of the foreign aid program, and so on.

I doubt that this point of view provides an acceptable prescription for the future, that the American people will agree with Senator Ferguson that the best gear in which to move into their future is reverse. New problems will call for new methods, for practical empiricism in political approach to them, for imagination and daring and common sense. They will call for a yet undiscovered reconciliation between the problems of bigness and a society dedicated to the dignity and worth of the individual. The development of "automation" in industry has perhaps only just begun. It may be that our already vast national production can continue to even greater volume with no more, or even fewer people to operate the machines. And yet our population is steadily increasing; 800,000 to 1,000,000 new workers enter the ranks of the employable every year.

[3] The Honorable Herbert Hoover, *op. cit.*, p. A3961.

Here, perhaps, is a new field for management of the thrust of forces by a government conceived of as the whole people organized to do what needs to be done. How, I do not know. But it seems plain that a vast amount of non-profit-yielding production of wealth— wholly apart from defense—is essential to an educated democracy, living a rounded and healthy life, and playing a worthy part in helping other peoples achieve the same goals. By 1970 our college-age population presenting themselves for higher education will have nearly doubled, and the need for additional plant and teachers will be enormous. The problem of overcrowded elementary and secondary schools is already upon us. So is the need for roads and the redevelopment of cities in the light of modern traffic and the movement to the suburbs of industry, commerce, and population. Recreational facilities, so essential to health and happiness, are a necessity, hardly less urgent than the availability of medical care.

The emerging problem does not seem to be that our society will be glutted with the production of material things, but whether some of our vast energy can be directed to producing these non-profit-yielding requirements of a good life. To do this wisely will require the highest political ingenuity, for the task bristles with problems of governmental management, of federal-state relationships, of dangers of governmental interference beyond the point of necessity, of the aggrandizement of the state. For instance, if it becomes necessary to double the provision for higher education, in plant and teachers, does anyone believe that this can be done by private benevolence? If government assistance is necessary, then what government, federal, state, or municipal, or combinations of them? If these governments provide the bulk of the funds, do they control the education? These questions go to the heart of a free and progressive society.

We should not be overawed, but challenged. The challenge has to be met by thought and effort, by a willingness to experiment and a desire to preserve. It cannot be met by formulae, whether a formula by which these tasks are carried on by private enterprise, or must be self-supporting, or one by which the welfare state would undertake them all. Ingenuity equal to that which created the electronic brain, applied with the same concentrated vigor to these problems, can and will solve them, though the electronic brain cannot.

If we look beyond our borders, as we did earlier in this volume, at the prospect before us, it is undoubtedly stern but not disheartening. The materials in resources, intelligence, and friends are available to us to create and maintain a balance of power which can safely support the adjustments, relaxation of immediate dangers and tensions, and the settlements of differences which will enable us to live through the hazards of the present without disaster, to come through the winter of the Cold War into a warmer and more promising spring. Certainly we are not in the grip of an ice age with the environment frozen and immovable. There is movement; and the movement is capable of being channeled to safe and constructive purposes.

The hazards of the future in our foreign relations do not lie, so it seems to me, in an intractable environment or in lack of means. They lie elsewhere, and chiefly in the realm of mind and will. Can we keep the hard realities clearly before us, and not deceive ourselves into believing that the facts are as we so much wish them to be? Have we the will and constancy to keep on doing what needs to be done when it involves foregoing, in the present, things that we would like to have and do and say, for the sake of the future? Have we the necessary powers of self-discipline? For in our democracy there is no one but ourselves to discipline us. If we do not do it, only the consequence of our folly can. Then it will be too late.

Mr. Molotov posing for the photographers in a ten-gallon hat, Mr. Molotov with the new smile, Mr. Molotov appreciating American art shows the Soviet state in infinitely better guise than Mr. Molotov leading the "hate America" chorus. The change is not without significance; nor is the change from the policy which led to the attack on Korea to the policy which led to the meeting of the heads of states without significance. This is movement. But changed aspects and changed policies must not obscure the reality of the power relationships which under-lie changed aspects and changed policies. However affable a face the Soviet state shows to the world, we would make a grave mistake to co-operate in a shift of power in favor of the Communist system, either by action or inaction. Negotiation and adjustment of conflicts are the ends to-ward which much sacrifice and effort have gone, but we must never lose sight of what we are negotiating about or the effect of adjustments on power relationships.

If we act with common sense and restraint and no nonsense, we can come through the troublous years. I have no lack of faith in the ability of our democracy and of those working toward the same ends to do the needful; neither do I think that it will be easy for us or them. Among other things, we must all school ourselves to be less volatile, not to swing high with hope and swing low with disappointment and pessimism. Indeed some of us seem to be attempting the difficult feat of swinging both ways at the same time. We rush to read or listen to the weekly press conferences. Are the prospects of peace up or down this Wednesday? If the news report does not give a clear answer, perhaps our favorite columnist or commentator will. The real movements take place more slowly than this. We distract ourselves, impair the con-stancy of our wills, by too much inquiry into the omens.

I do not share the view, or the resigned hopelessness which it seems to inspire, that modern democracies with their mass electorates cannot stay the course against the tauter, more constant pressure of the monolithic state. For one thing they have done so. Hitler, Mussolini, and Tojo were not successes who ought to make us despair of our own methods. And I venture to say that whatever worrying goes on in Washington, or London, can be matched in Moscow or Peiping. It is a common failing to exaggerate our adversary's strategy and ability to execute it. Surely, a large electorate presents more problems and is harder to inform and persuade than a small one. The interests of the voters are more varied, so is their education, their standards of judgment, so is their attention to the political debate. The task of organization is larger and more complicated as the electorate grows. But these difficulties do not daunt a leader with courage and a zest and knack for the art of politics; nor do all the media for influencing mass opinion—the press, the radio, and television. Perhaps the odds are still on the side of the heavier battalions, but the odds can be wrong, as Mr. Truman showed in 1948. The voters, too, are often wrong; but it is grave error to conclude from this that they cannot be right and are not capable of pretty shrewd discrimination, or that there is any better or safer judgment which can be sought.

We tend, I think, to be too self-conscious, too self-analytical, to turn to the pollsters to find out for whom we are going to vote or what we are going to do. Taking our own temperatures continually makes for morbidity and undermines the capacity to act. Some time ago advertisements called attention to a type of dress for women known as "Spectator Sports." Being an onlooker had become enough of an institution to call for distinctive dress. The late Frank Simonds told me a story, which he insisted wryly was expressive of his point of view. He was attending a funeral. At the church door an usher approached him. "Are you a bearer, Mr. Simonds?" he was asked. "No," was the answer, "I'm a mourner."

Onlooking and mourning have their places. But in the workings of our democracy the great call and need is for participants. I could never regard salvation by faith and salvation by works as a dichotomy. It has always seemed to me that a vibrant and energetic faith produced works. And perhaps it happens the other way too. "Man," said Justice Holmes, ". . . is born to act. To act is to affirm the worth of an end, and to persist in affirming the worth of an end is to make an ideal."[4] So it is in life and in that important branch of life which is politics. One lives in action.

I have found a full and satisfying life of action in the fellowship of the Democratic party, with its deep roots in our American traditions and our profoundest beliefs about the nature of man and the functions of govern-

[4] Oliver Wendell Holmes, speech to the Class of '61 at the 50th Anniversary of Graduation, June 28, 1911. *Speeches* (Little, Brown, and Company, Boston, 1934), pp. 95, 96-97.

ment, with its virility, its ever-renewed youth, its response to new problems and welcome to new ideas and methods. I believe that in this fellowship we can best serve the deepest needs of our country and of that larger civilization of which it is a part; and have tried to set forth the reasons for that belief. If the reader agrees and acts on his agreement, I shall be happy. If he disagrees, I shall not be unhappy, provided only that he acts, pulls his full weight in the boat, whether it is ours or the other. These are years of decision which will not come again. The need is for doers of the word and not hearers only.